RENEWALS 691-4574

DATE DUE

OCT 02			

Demco, Inc. 38-293

HARD COUNTRY

HARD COUNTRY

•

Sharon Doubiago

West End Press • Minneapolis • 1982

Some of these poems have been or will be published in *Alcatraz, Alchemy, Amerus, Beatitude, Beloit Poetry Journal, Big River News, Coast Peddler, Compages III, Dalmo'ma, Folio One, Frammis, Free Poems for the People, Ghost Dance, Greenfield Review, Himma, Home Planet News, Mendocino Arts and Entertainment Magazine, Mendocino Grapevine, NOWA, River Styx, Samzidat, Silver Vain, Sonoma County Stump, Tinderbox, Tioyabi Indian Anthology,* and *Total Abandon.* Poems have also appeared in **Western Edge: 33 Poets** (Ten Mile River Press), **Peace Is Our Profession** (East River Anthology Press), **Works** (ed. Dan Propper), and **Family Violence: Poems on the Pathology** (Moonlight Publications). **Visions Of A Daughter Of Albion** is a chapbook printed by Ten Mile River Press, 1979. An earlier version of the title poem "Hard Country" was printed as a broadside by West End Press, 1981.

This volume is sponsored by Midwest Villages and Voices.
For information, write:
Midwest Villages and Voices
3451 Cedar Avenue South
Minneapolis, MN 55407

The publication of this book was supported in part by a grant from Meridel Le Sueur

A WEST END PRESS publication
under the supervision of
John Crawford, editor, and
Anya Achtenberg, associate editor.

ISBN 0-931122-25-2

West End Press
P.O. Box 7232
Minneapolis, MN 55407

Photo credit: Paul Reynolds

Cover design: Tree Swenson

CONTENTS

Part I, HEADSTONE

Part II, HEADLAND

Part III, HEARTLAND

Part IV, HEARTSEA

To my mother and father who have taught me the land
To my son and daughter, Danny and Shawn, who have taught me history
To my sister and brother, Donna and Clarke, who share this story
To my nieces and nephew, Tanya, Dondi, Chelli, Christy and Erinn,
with love for hope

To create a new desire: To remember the dismembered

—Meridel Le Sueur

Part I
HEADSTONE

HEADSTONE, I

Headstone: for Lucile Edens Walton (1907-1978), my grandmother's oldest child, who died, suddenly, this week as I write this, who is remembered still as the most beautiful girl in Ducktown, Tennessee, who three days before she died told her preacher of a dream. She was in a large stadium and she saw Papa. She started running to him but he disappeared. Then she saw him again, looking at her from the crowd. She ran to him, calling *Papa! Papa!* but he disappeared again. And this occurred over and over.

Because my father calls me Lu, for her

And for my Uncle K.D., Kermit David Edens (1911-1977), because I promised.

Signal Hill

My father leaves us in the car
and drinks beer in the Hilltop Bar.
The red neon woman who wears only
a ruffled apron and high heels
carries a tray of drinks
around and around the top of the hill
to the giant robots that pump
the fields.

In her red light my baby
brother and sister in the backseat of the car
are contorted in screams Daddy doesn't hear
over the jukebox and high squeals
of the bar maid I never see and wonder
if she too wears no clothes.
I hear her cry ah Babes!
We come here every Friday when he gets paid
but my brother and sister are still afraid
of the nodding creatures in the dark
we are parked between.

The city spreads beneath us
in a rainbow-spilled oil puddle.
The harbor is lit with battleships
that strain at their ropes
toward bigger war across the sea.

The dirty men keep driving up beside us.
I sit in the mother's seat
and they say to me the things men say
to mothers.

I study her gay nipples
and wonder if mine will get that way.
Far below, on the shore of the Pike
a man sits on top of the neon needle
for months just to break a record.
One man says of him as he runs
his middle finger across the dewy window
of my face,
Tough, not gettin any.

When Daddy comes through the door
beneath the spinning neon lady
it is the only time I ever see him
happy. Now we drive the cold side
of Signal Hill, the backside of the city and sea
so dark even now in the middle of the twentieth century
they hide the dying, the ones
they still can't cure, my mother
in her sanitarium.

We drive across the starry oil field
to her window where she lies
in the contagion ward we kids cannot go near.
My father taps on her dark window
and soon my mother lifts the glass
and puts her porcelain hand
out into the dark for him.

He puts one of his
on one of her large breasts
that are not like the red neon woman's
and sometimes lays his head
on her white arm that knows no sun
and between the groans of the field
letting go its oil
I hear him sigh
oh, honey, *and sometimes*
jesus

1.   Eden Stone

The broad human head
and shoulders rise from the forest floor.
The nose, the mouth, the eyes
look from the ridge out over the land
that has disappeared beneath the waters
of Dale Hollow Lake on the mid-
Tennessee-Kentucky line

and the words

E. Edens, age 94, English
died
1558

2.   Who

They keep testing the headstone
and keep finding
the stone native to the area
and the writing as old as it claims

30 years before
Sir Walter Raleigh's
Lost Colony
on the Carolina shore

50 years
before Jamestown

3.   "the ancient light of the ground"

Beneath the Continent's skin
the ancient light of the earth
tells the story of a fair-skinned people
living among the Indians
a story that goes back to the first pioneers

Eight days down the Tennessee
lives a white people
who have long beards and whiskers
and wear clothing.

Bardic accounts say "children of the Welsh rovers"
led by Prince Madoc in the 1100s
crossed the Atlantic to the Gulf
ascended the Mississippi to the Tennessee
and settled the Highland.

Who are the Melungeons?
Why is there a statue to Madoc
at the entrance to Mobile Harbor?

What is the origin
of the 12th Century Welsh fort
at Manchester, Tennessee,
the ancient Hebrew coins
excavated in Eastern Kentucky?

4.   Story Teller

The blood complicates the hair, the yellow curls
like a discarded sunflower
pitched weeks ago from the green stalk
onto the dark forest floor.

The blood still remembers its heleotropic path,
the procession behind the torches of the universe,
and the sound of the air
buffeted by its movement
is a hymn

I am five, standing at the window
on the corner of Roosevelt and Industrial
looking out to the neighborhood.
The members of my family
are in the room behind me.

At the north end of Industrial
Mt. Wilson rises snowcapped in the San Gabriels
over the Los Angeles basin

that mountain, Mama says, *keeps my sanity*
the only reason
I can stand this

I am looking out to the street
when in a skyblue Santana moment
the sky comes inside and I am miles
within my face and hair
that grow larger than the window
and frame as I stand here
our little stucco house south of Los Angeles
and all of us in it
and all the neighbors on our street
after World War II

I understand, in this moment of wind

I understand we are each stranded
in our essential Body,
my mother, my father, my sister, my brother
the neighbors, all
the people, myself

I understand we come from a truth
we each wholly and separately possess
to a particular house and street in time
to tell the story only our body knows

and our tragedy will be
we will not tell it well
because our witnesses
will be telling their stories

Each will call
the Lover to her place:
each will know
the inadequacy of the mother
each will know
the cruelty of the father
each will seek
the lover who seeks
to tell her
all she cannot hear

and all cruelty and evil between people is this
though the world
waits for us to arrive at its shore
though our life depends on it
our death will finally be
the place we could never go
the story we couldn't enter

I am large within my head that frames the window
and I understand evil
is in not understanding this

We expect the others
to live our story

I am five, I will never understand
why we are stranded in our selves
but in this moment I know
my own story
is understanding our singleness
that I am destined to move my body and time
into the body-time
the story
of Others.

5.

And the Mississippi flowed
backwards five days

before I was born my body
as maize

Who were the men and women
who prepared the ground
by making love on it
which made the songs run
from field to field

Who were the women
who then worked the corn
in the fields
owned only by women

my body, the wife of a king, tattooed,
carried on a throne
by four painted braves
cooled by peacock fans

preceded by hornblowers, followed
by the parade

on the way to the war
party

Who were the men
owned by the mothers

Who was the mother-in-law
never allowed to see the man
who took her daughter

Whose were the scalps
that decorated his staff

Who were the women
who tortured the boy
tied to a pole in the center of town
who sang his war song
to show his superior courage
who tried not to break
before he died

my body painted
a confederacy of red and white towns
that sang the Cherokee chants
of war and peace

Who was the supreme chief of the
"beloved occupation"
War, with an eagle for his head,
my white body

as place
of sanctuary

city of refuge
for those who fled
blood avengers
who were those
who might find
asylum

before I was born the Cherokee
who slipped away from the trail
of tears and all the dying
into the hills of North Carolina
and Tennessee

Before I was born my body
the wife Daniel Boone
mistook for a deer

6.

I was born a dead infant and buried
as the boundary line of a great nation
torn asunder by the earthquake
that heralded the coming of white
men that caused the Mississippi to flow
backwards five days

and when I rose to look at you
coming through the gap
I knew myself as old

and when I rose
the mountain I had been
heaved and collapsed
into an ancient crater

and I knew I would forever now be
the gap
to be filled

7.

Who was the boy
who rode the back of the beast
over the roots and stumps
so the father could hold the plow

Who were the women
who told their stories
to each other across the hills
by the rhythm of the pounding of the corn

Who were the Nordic
hiding in Scotland
sent into Ireland as protestants
to influence the Catholics

who then left for America as Scotch-Irish
as medieval Wandering Baptists, these
people back of me

the English
who
came over with Lord Baltimore
150 years before the Revolution

Who came down into the Blue Ridge
built the first cabin

Who were the seven brothers
who settled South Carolina
Who was Jacob Edens who first went down
to Alabama, then up
to Middle Tennessee

Who were the ones for the Revolution
added an 's' to Eden,
many Gardens, they wanted Democracy

Who signed his name largest
on the Declaration of Independence
Who told me a Hancock married a Corn
a Corn married a Chitwood
a Chitwood married an Edens

Who was the Reverend James Edens
at the Battle of Kings Mountain
who brought his congregation into the Wautauga
who founded the Sinking Creek Baptist Church
in the Saddle of the Gap

Who all were named for Francis Marion
The Swamp Fox of South Carolina

Who were the soldiers
who while campaigning
located homesites

lured by the cheap price
$99 down, don't have to pay
till '79

Who felt pinned to Virginia
the despised aristocracy

the 20,000 who filed through
the Gap, the Wilderness Way
in one generation
for 200 years the Great
Barrier, valleys leading
nowhere, scattered tales
of the storied
Blue Grass, the Sweet
Water

Who was captured by the blackened
Dragging Canoe and Old Abraham
as they stole up the Nolichuckey

Who took her to the Cherokee Red Town
bound her to the stake to burn

Who lived for 20 years not a day safe
from *lurking savages*
their *sadistic torture*

Who
wanted this land
that much?

          In the Hall of Dreams near Chattanooga
          the treacherous Dragging Canoe
          founded a new tribe, the Chickamauga

          and later runaway slaves
          hid there
          and later
          in the stalagmites
          the Confederates

Who fought the Battle of the Clouds
directly above
the Frozen Niagara

Who crawled home to you

sitting in the farmhouse
when the battle took place, all sides
Franklyn County, Tennessee
soaked in blood

Who fought for the North
came home the enemy
even to his wife

who then took up with the maid
Who are the cousins they birthed
you wouldn't claim

Who are the Black people
who look like us

Who was the rich aunt
Mary Sharp
who told you to write
after she went blind
who then went broke
to send her slaves
to Liberia, Africa

In the Hall of Dreams
near the old homestead
draperies of violet, arctic
blue

hundreds of capillaries
a million years

before I was born my body as
cornfields your Daddy plowed
who fainted in the fields
a stroke of the sun
blinding his mind

to Who
he was

the family disease, amnesia
Chitwoods can't take the sun
you told me, not enough potassium
in the blood

your chore as a girl
to watch him, *George Washington*
Chitwood as he plows
Edens' Hollow of the Elk

you follow way behind
so he won't be reminded
carrying sugar
salt.

8.   Chitwood

You were a map, Grandma
to a place I couldn't find
born in a land without roots
to a family with amnesia
who came to the basin without weather
to start over

The roads you told me you walked as a girl
are under water now, the old place
in your diary you return to
on the road in your dreams

Waited on the river bank each day
after teaching school
for your father to come in the buggy
to take you home

it grows dark
the stars wake from their dreams

and the *light*
you write of the cottonmouth
infested Elk River you swim in
is heaven's light
the year after your sister
drank of it and died

and your brother on the trestle siding
of the bridge they were building
across the Arkansas
when the first train came through

who fell into the river when the bridge collapsed
breaking his neck between two rocks

1904, you were in love
with *Marion Avon Edens*
of Lynchburg, Tennessee
who was gone out west to Arizona
who kept sending you the money to come

Finally you packed. They took you to the train.
You wouldn't get on. To this day they laugh
you couldn't leave your mother.
But 1904: I bring the year and the stories together
to a story never told

your mother Nancy
who never recovered.
Ida and Will
dead from the rivers.

She used to sit and rock
seeing way off
never acknowledge nothing

Who is it that she sees
Who is it that I look just like

Who are you?
the schoolteacher in this photograph
of fifty children
body and face of my own I am named for
Tura Lura Lura, born
on your birthday, all of you dead
barefoot babies, teenage boys, you
at the door, your arm on your hip
a fierce boredom on your face

or is it anger? or is it grief? or is it all of these?
Who came on Wednesday evenings in the buggy
to take you to prayer meeting

Who finally came home from Arizona
wearing a Navajo chief's robe
who spent the next forty years in the dark
drifts of the mine

because you wouldn't leave the land you loved
or your mother

Who always said *it's the Edens*
in you
Grandma, *you* weren't an Edens
How long it has taken me to understand
Chitwood, Lura Maude
named for the Maude of two poets
and your mother, Nancy
daughter of Macaja P. *Reagin* and Jane
Goodloe

It is *my* mother in whom the squaws live
Squaw, the only name on the marriage certificates
Squaw: Cherokee, *Squaw:* Seminole, *Squaw:* Choctaw
It is my mother, who is not
your daughter
who says now that I have your trunk
she will come down and tell me who
the people are in it

You and my mother, neither of you Edens
who carry their history, as you carried
the strangers, the children
against the fathers' amnesia.

9. *The Linga Sharira*

I pulled the trunk in a trailer
from Ramona to Mendocino, your trunk
25 years under the house, the trunk
brought by train to California, the trunk
against amnesia, the family disease.

On the forgotten 25th anniversary of your death
I put the trunk at the foot of my bed.

I lie down.
You ride in the backseat of the black limousine
and pass before me. You stare at me fiercely
from the same unyielding socket of bone.
Your face in the window
is too large
even in death.

It is the first time
I see you.
I had forgotten your face.
In the morning I find a friend dead.
In a week your daughter.

10.   *the devastation that goes on*

Who were the lovers
who went to Ducktown
to leave 40 years later
eroded, as stripped of life
as the copper basin

a convulsive red scar, the place
my father has no memory of

Grandpa, a hardrock miner
copper   lead   zinc
foreman, running jack hammers
down the drifts

Years he never saw the sun
Went down before the sun came up
Came up after the sun went down

Sometimes, Grandma, you walked to the Georgia border.
I make it up. You must have walked
to North Carolina looking for a tree.
How else did you bear
that poisoned corner of Tennessee?
Or did you forget too
about green, your husband crawling
beneath all borders
deep in the earth's mind
the light on his forehead
leading the way

and five children crawling through you.
You never healed, you told me,
the Edens' head too large.
Light and air could enter you, the pain
worse than birth

my father, the last baby
when Grandpa came home again from Arizona,
home from the only job he could get
with his crippled leg. *Hangman.* Better
to hack away in the graves of Tennessee.

Daddy
who thought the whole earth
without trees, without flowers, without grass
the way it's supposed to be, he thought, death-cracked

blood-red   rain-rotted   tree-split   body-ripped   hillskulls

who swam in a green river of cupric chloride
and copperheads
who has no memory

of four boys, two of them twins
and the fifth, the oldest
the most beautiful girl in Ducktown
Daddy called me Lu for
wandering bare hills
coming home covered in red dirt

finding tomahawks every time
they went out the door
dropped for eons in a forest
no longer there

Arizona in Tennessee

and Grandpa's last job in the Changing House
where they changed their clothes to go down

then the strikes he
believed in
like religion

Who was the son
who came home sterile
from atomic testing in the Pacific
still a company man
to talk him out of the strike

the twin who loved you
who hated his father for being a union man
until *I came to know him*
on his death bed

who failed and left
on your 60th birthday
who took Mama and Daddy
back across the country

who left a year to the day before I was born

the place your son, my father
has no memory of
though he lived there
until a man

        Lost Silver Mines
        somewhere, the Ruby Caverns
        the Tennessee Shaft
        3.8 million tons
        extracted, the Copper Basin, Copper
        Hill, by the underground
        stoping method

the place of silence where there are no birds
the place where there are no seeds, only scars
of your having been there
a wide red-rock copper river
named for a chief named Duck
whose trees are gone, who now is lost, whose babies
crying in the kudsu
crawl back onto the hills
who drank the river and died
who drowned in the Tennessee River project

Who said you were the most beautiful woman he'd ever seen
as you departed the door of the company store
he was coming in

Who was the god
they complain you prayed to
continuously

Who was killed on your road by the town's first automobile

What did my father do at sixteen
so terrible it is the only line
scratched in the diary you kept
your whole life

who then burst out of there
caught a freight to Walla Walla
to make the wheat harvest
who wrote back *don't worry Ma,
love, the black sheep of the family*

Who addressed you from Memphis different ways
Lura, Maude, Sister, and in some
Sweetheart

who had *the biggest hands on any man ever seen*
your brother
dead in a collision
at a Miami intersection
but when they dug him up
for the investigation
a bullet was found in his head

    11.   The Secret Writer

They lost the strike.
When the killing was over
he was too old to work,
the hope for a pension gone.

I open the trunk.
A letter from the company headquarters in Minneapolis,
*Sorry, Mrs. Edens, we have no coverage
for silicosis.*

A postcard of Los Angeles County General Hospital
where poor Avon lay 5 months
and died 1948
where I lay twenty years later
hemorrhaging from an abortion in Watts
not knowing who
also died here

Sewn into the lining of her Sunday blackbeaded purse
Some of Avon's Last Words To Me
trying to get comfortable, the pain
worse than breathing

I pulled the cover up and tucked it about his neck
"You need me don't you to keep you covered?"
He said O Yes!
I did the usual turns for him
putting hair tonic on his head.
I said, "Avon, we have a better home
than this, haven't we?"
He bowed his head in reply and said
"Isn't this the day you are taking me home?"

12.   Grandpa   Who It Is My Brother Takes After

I sit beside him as he rides me in his new electric car
open to the high palms that line Paramount Boulevard
Mama says they'll cut down soon to widen the road.
He calls me *Goldilocks.*

We sit on the cement porch steps on Roosevelt
Mama earned the $99 down for by waitressing the graveyard shift
to watch the ants swarm out of the new crack
because the earth has moved
and they're free now to live.

Daddy got on at Douglas
tells me men want to leave the earth behind.
Daddy, the baby, the poorest,
brought you west where the earth
quakes and you saw the ocean
the first time at 68.

Chickens in the backyard, a garden he plows
until the new ordinances, and Grandpa's last job
as night watchman across the tracks
I learn left and right by facing. I still
turn my body to face the passing train
to know my direction.
One night he drew the Bear
in the sky for me

and reached for me too old the last time I saw him alive
reached down from the high quilts and Tennessee
while I clung to the leather strop on the door
he slapped his razor on
Goldilocks, Goldilocks
come here Goldilocks

the words like tiny trapped miners
drowning in the blood of his throat
and when I held his hand and still he called
Goldilocks. Come here, Goldilocks
the words like miners suffocating
in the copper fumes of his lungs
I knew I did not belong in this old dark house
that fit everyone's size
but my own

and in dreams I am Goldilocks still
wandering through cities and woods
searching for the place
that will fit me
just right, Goldilocks

the ache to be
Bear, little white person
without roots

13.

When he died Grandma we took you every Sunday
to his grave, though everyone said
he's really not here and you said
Soon we will all be together again
in the Glory Land and see Jesus
face to face.

But once I heard you say to the ground
I love you Avon. I'm weak. I'm trying
to keep my promise
not to dig you up.

I practiced my tap dancing around the letters
MARION AVON EDENS
a flat granite slab in the ground.
The modern way, Daddy said.

We flapped out the blanket over him.
I smoothed it of eucalyptus buttons.
We ate cold ham and cornbread and I watched
the curve in the road around the headstones.
It was the only park in our town
and all roads are straight
south of L.A.

I didn't let them see me watching him.
Sometimes the ground glowed and I could almost see
what he dreamed in the moley darkness
about himself and his own light,
a miner again deep in the earth.

The modern way, Daddy said,
but I wished he had a headstone
that rose from the ground
like the old one next to him I sat on
pretending it was him
riding his shoulders high in the palms
on the way to the sea.

14.

The day we followed you
with our lights
beneath the deadbone skull of sky
to Bellflower and Firestone
the palmtree park where Grandpa lay
I sat in the front seat with Daddy
and the mortuary man
who drove.

We came to a stop beneath Eucalyptus
that circled the County Farm.
A boy I recognized from junior high
crossed in front of us.
You and the whole procession waited
for this boy only I knew.
His hands were shoved deep into his pockets.
Mine came half-way to the window
but I saw he did not know me
in this black limousine.

I sat in the front row of Gloria Gardens
Missionary Baptist Church.
The preacher began the story
of Sister Edens.
The piano notes banged against the walls
and the congregation that sang
a thudding high-pitched echoing wail
that knocked water to my eyes
I controlled by watching
all I could see of you over the carnations:
the familiar, wild white hair
you always laughed you couldn't control.

We sang *all the saints adore thee.*
Cast down their golden crowns
around the glassy sea. For days now
I had wondered
how you die.

If I looked hard at you
deep within the cavedark of your wild white head
and not the preacher's story
I could control the glassy sea in my eyes.
Everyone I knew was here
except those at school
who would not know me.
I don't know why I was wild with the effort
not to let anyone see me cry.
For days I had wanted to know *why*
you lived. And why, then,
you lived such boring years.

I was the last person in the long shuffling line
to view you
before they shut the coffin.

The piano cried.
Your hair was sprayed blue, controlled
with nets.
Someone had made a dumb painting of you
on your face.

15.   Hollydale

Men circled a red-throbbing fire
deep inside the factory
making toilets on the street you died on
in the middle of the twentieth century.
Shook and jabbed their burning tools
at the boys who played outside.

Coals dumped from trains
before the war were caves we made forts in.
Sage and tumbleweeds blew down Industrial Avenue
and old men, beards on knobby canes
they shook at the sky, growled and hobbled,
pushed funny wheels they sat on
from the County Farm

Rancho Los Amigos

Winos, the mothers named them
who hid in the tumbleweeds
who opened their pants to me
when I walked by

Mama said the first war
changed everything.
No one's been the same since.
They wore red poppies on their chests.
I won the poster contest: *the Poppy*

the first life that comes back
after a field
is soaked
in human blood.

16.   The Hall of Dreams A Million Years Before I Was Born

men circled a redthrobbing fire
in the feltboard flames of Hell
at Trinity Bible Church on Industrial,
the long block from our house you told me
my Daddy could swim that far underwater

and Billy Grahan screamed

Who will make you
fishers of men

in the tent next to our forts
we dug in earth and the boys took me down
and laid me in underground caves.
Their heads, a congregation circling my bent knees
looked for something way up
between my thighs, while I
looked inside the mind
of Earth.

17.   November 18, 1953: *The Linga Sharira*

The night you died
was my turn to sit with you
in your apartment on Industrial.
I stayed in the living room.
I pretended I did not feel you calling me
from your cold back room.
Or that I did not hear the walls and ceiling
banging down on your weak heart.
My own was lit
like the red pulse of the foundry fire
forging steel across the street.

Men were coming for the graveyard shift.
Your icebox dripped water.
I did my Bible work
as we had always done together,
In my Father's house are many mansions...
your beautiful old finger
leading me down the narrow path of words
the key to your house tied to it
with a blue ribbon.

Mama kept saying you had entered
Second Childhood. Everyone said
we were just alike.
I was born on your birthday,
I was named for you, *Lura*, a secret poet.
Once I saw you standing at Knott's Berry Farm
among the sunglassed cars.
I saw the sky move inside you
as it comes sometimes inside me,
blowing time around like a cloud.
You were a girl then
swimming the Elk River in Tennessee.

Each will call the Lover to her place:
You called me to your room.
The light is hurting my eyes, Sharon Lura.
Won't you please shut the crack in my curtain?

Outside men called to each other across the parking lot.
Car doors slammed shut.
I didn't look at you.
I pretended that closing off the light
was all you wanted.
You wanted me to talk to you.
You burned your eyes into my back.
I was memorizing another verse, *For death*
is come up into our windows...oh, Grandma, this
particular house and street in time
where you lay bearing down forever into its darkness,
is mine, my terror
of the body, my terror
of meeting you.

I hurried back across the linoleum
flowered eternity of your room and your sudden
command
that I look
to the dark corner
where you lay.

You were poured out like water
into the long white river banks of your hair
I had never seen let flow.
You had come to the window
of your strange body
to me for the first time.
But I fled, I withheld love,
I was too small.

Mama relieved me.
I ran home across the lawns.
Beneath the street lamp an old man
drinking whiskey hissed after me,
Fuck, he said, *Blondie*
come here!

And then I saw you the next day
coming down Roosevelt in the car with Mama
as I was coming down Wilson with my girlfriend.
It had been an amazing day.
In the library I had become lost
for the first time in what I now know
was art, a strange exhilaration
I'd only known before in prayer.
I wanted to take the stallions into my arms,
as now, walking with her on the street, my friend.
And I couldn't stop laughing.
I knew you'd get well.

But as the car approached
you were really Billy Jean.
"I thought you were Grandma. You looked just like her."
And Mama is saying from the window
Grandma died last night, Sharon Lura.

I couldn't stop laughing to my girlfriend.
And Billy Jean I thought was you
coming down to Ramona the next year
with her new fiance
passed a car on Imperial
which suddenly dipped into ground fog.
They never saw the diesel.
Uncle K.D., who lost his mother and his daughter
within a year, told me
it happened so fast
she was still smiling at him
though every bone in her face
was broken.

    18.   Ramona

We moved to the country
to start over. Daddy said
to get me away from the pachucos
who love blondes. *Ramona,*
named for the girl who married an Indian

and because he went fishing in the Sierras
the week after you died.
He was climbing a hill and when he came to the crest
the sky went inside him.
Time blew around like a cloud
and he saw the earth for the first time.
She was green, not red.

> Who came to my mother
> in the garden in Ramona
> told her to write
> a letter to her sister

And she went up to the house
and wrote
like automatic writing
and mailed it to Chattanooga
and doesn't remember
what you told her

19. Ramon

I love an Indian boy, Ramon
whose tribe of the Colorado River, *Mojave*,
are Geographers and Dreamers.

Ramon climbs the pepper tree to my window.
My father is in the next room.
He puts his tongue between my teeth.
He makes circles on my belly with his hands,
whispers *I love you, I love you.*
I see the earth for the first time as if I have left.
Tidal waves of ocean
come into the desert. I leap
from childhood's impotency
to his dark hand on my breast.

I want to ask you who watches us
from the Glory Land

Who is it I am so like?

Ramon hides in the hills at night.
The sheriff is looking for him.
Questions me. Daddy hits me
across the garden he is plowing
in April, on my 13th birthday,
the first one you miss.
Mama says he's jealous and I'm too beautiful.
I understand.
But it's more than he dreams

I see people reaching out for me,
geographers and dreamers
in the hot milk he spills on my belly.
They are trying to tell me their story
before they drown.
I wanted to know, Grandma,
how you bore your dull life.

Now I know.

HEADSTONE, II
AMERICAN ALCHEMY

There are in Japan old documents, copied from older documents... which give a history of the world going back not thousands of years but tens of thousands of years. They describe epochs, periods, hundreds of dynasties, their rise and fall, the spread of the five colored races, the changing land masses, a planetary network stretched across the planet. Then, 12,000 years ago, a great cataclysm struck, the moon was stuck in the sky, the sun disappeared, the waters rose, and tidal waves obliterated great coastal cities; currents changed, the weather grew colder, crops failed, and prosperity ceased. Civilizations failed, farmers turned to hunters, people huddled, struck dumb in awe and fear. Finally, according to these documents, the "people" set out upon the ocean in boats to look for their "lost culture." They never returned. Perhaps human beings have been wandering and looking for the lost culture, their lost origins even since....

Paul Hawken
"Long Before Columbus, the Buddhist Discovery of America"

"I thought of Jung who said his clients dreamed most often of the movie 'Hiroshima, Mon Amour' and that in the dream the couple had to connect in order that the bomb not be dropped."

Man and His Symbols
M.L. von Franz

No hay patria, hay tierra, imagenes de tierra,
polvo y luz en el tiempo....

Octavio Paz

PART I   RAMONA

1.   Fatherland

A thousand years ago the Vietnamese
wrote with honey
words on the leaves of their native trees
and then turned a thousand
caterpillars into the trees
who ate the honey
and the leaves beneath the honey.

Then when the conquering Chinese
again came down the trail
the trees were full of windtossed, shimmering
leafy words
that turned them in terror and awe
back to their own country.

2.   Fusang: A Map   (The Buddhist Discovery of America)

In the second year of the period
"Great Brightness"
499 a.d.
a band of Buddhist monks
led by Hwui Shan
sailed east from China
20,000 li into the rising sun.

The place they came to
on the North American continent
still carries the name of Hwui.
At Port Hueneme the people greeted
the immigrants from the land
west of the sun
as holy men and adopted
their Buddha ways.

From Port Hueneme the band proceeded
south along the coast
to the basin where tar boils.
Crossing the borax deserts
with shallow lakes the color of milk
descending the "Great Luminous Canyon,"
they came to the Hopi
who themselves had come
from the land west of the sun, then walked
to the four doors of the continents,
to the North Pole, to the South Pole
to the ocean on the East
their paths beating
the Great Cross into the land
to find the Crossroads
at Four Corners, the Center
of Fusang, Land of the Oak, the New World.

31

Following the Hopi Trail
the band of Buddhist monks
descended south into Mexico

and everywhere they went

bearded white men on canes
clad in long robes, appearing
suddenly and mysteriously
upon the places of the people

their appearance was recorded
in legend, art, and religion

Quetzacoatl in Cholua,
Votan in Chiapas,
Zamna and Kukulcan in Yucatan,
Gucumatz in Guatemala,
Viracocha in Peru,
Sume and Paye-Tome in Brazil,
the Mysterious Apostle in Chile,
the Bochica in Columbia

and the route can still be taken
by following the places of his name
Hwui Shan,
the places of his mendicant title,
pi-kui,

and the places named for *Saka,*
the name of Buddha:

from Port *Hue*neme to *Saca*ton, Arizona
down through Mexico to Guatemala and north again
the cities of

*Wicam, Hue*tama, *Huichol, Hui*zontla, *Huepac, Hui*la,
*Saca*ton, *Zaca*tlan, *Zaca*tecas, *Zaca*tepec, *Saca*bchen, *Zaca*pa, and
*Pica*cho, *Pic*hucalco, *Pica*ho, *Picchu,*

and finally
Guatema-la
the place of Prince Guatama,
the Buddha.

3.   Ramona

Driven from mountain valley to mountain valley
by the Whites hungry for their land

the couple settled on the peak of Mt. San Jacinto,
the furthest exile, the highest wall
between desert and sea.

And there the Cahuilla lost his mind.
Every wisp of cloud was the Whites
in pursuit of him, coming for
his wife, the white woman.
Deer, hawk, mountain lion told him
they had found his mind, but they ate it.

When his murderer blew off his face
after he was already dead, Ramona
scattered his pieces to the four warm corners:
desert, mountain, basin, sea, naming
with flesh and story, this last edge
of country.

Then she lay on her back along the southern rim.
Her silver hair fell as granite
all the way to Mexico,
where the mountains, standing in thought,
turned blue to honor her.

She is the one who hides her name
in every arroyo and chaparral wash,
like the Egyptian sungod that bears her name,
Amon-ra. Like Isis in search
of her lover who is strewn in pieces
over the land, in tar, lupine, acorn oak,
in golden poppies that fold around him
at the approach of stars.

Ramona is her white man's name.
The Indians won't tell her real name.
But someday soon she will rise from her sleep.
When this happens, her husband, the land
will once again be theirs.

4.   Marcelene

He awakens you from the abortion you never dreamed you'd have
You awaken from the autopsy you never wanted them to perform
He informs you the knife slipped
something slipped, something has gone wrong, you must
sign your name, your address, is it
America?   Switzerland?   Viet Nam?   where is the home
you knew?
your uterus has been punctured. invaded
you must sign the papers to remove it. or die
you have been invaded
the refugee coming down from the north has been. lost
you are drifting days in great danger

in a small sampan on the South China Sea

5. Nga-my

Nga-my says I have jewelry I have gold
Nga-my says I hardly knew a war was going on

Nga-my says I was top gymnast in Viet Nam   Nga-my says
        my family aristocratic

Nga-my has her abortion in private hospital says
        only recently lost my chastity

Nga-my says I will make my sponsor comfortable, that
        is my duty

To my sister Nga-my says
You are first American I see who is pretty
Americans are so so ugly. ugly.

My sister is on the phone with her famous Hollywood lover
Always there is about my sister the hint of high fame
her platinum hair, her red lips, her white shorts
Nga-my petting her, stroking her back, stroking her arms

so pretty.   always happy.   Marilyn Monroe.

6. *Nixon*

In a land hard to love, in a harsh, masculine land
this was the first, these rhythmic, low-wide mesas
coming west from the mountains we lived in as girls
down to the sea, the first land I loved. Mesas,
tables carved by saltmarsh lagoons, backwaters,
and the eternal systolic wash from Asia.

The car fills
with Viet Nam, Cambodia
the language, the images, the stories

of prostitutes
who, upon arrival at Camp Pendleton
set up business
delighted to be
in this mythic place
source of the Americans.
They call it *Paradise*
in Vietnamese

while the Pacific splashes blue to the end of the Western World
to the only land on this coast not sliced
filled or blocked, nor oranges drying
in the groves to be plowed under
for new homes: the only land saved
has been saved by the Marines
to practice the Kill.

Who lives for the poem that can write everyone's exile home?
Hirschman asks, so I write this in verse, this letter to you
as a poem, this news story, these many stories, this essay,
this spilling and collecting of my life in these hills.
The details are ominous, journalistic, the experience
deepest poetry: how the San Onofre Nuclear Generating Station
and Richard Nixon
share the south and north rim of the lagoon
down in which
the refugees and marines are camped,
at the mouth of which
beneath this bridge we cross over,
Mexican farmworkers are bent
all in a row
for our food.

We are blonde, we are never stopped at the border
checking stations, though I wonder
of everyone's exile here
where during the war I passed and saw
a doomed California Brown Pelican
rowing her prehistoric, now DDT lope
between the San Clemente White House
and the weeping juices of the setting sun.
Then drove all night east to your house, Ramona,
and saw silhouetted in the sun as it rose
over Arizona
a fiery accident of two diesels
cracked like the egg shells of polluted pelicans
and I knew
this is almost
incredible. This
is an omen.

The radio tells that his first venture in months from his estate
was marred when he witnessed a freeway accident.
Three marines were killed. He directed traffic,
administered aid until help came.
The incident is reported
to have affected him deeply.

El Camino Real Exit, where he lives
he was always proud to point out,
his obvious bravura, his complete faith,
on the very ground of nuclear power.
But guards and gates now line both sides, the old King's Road,
the Spanish gates we swung on as girls
when we camped here, now the new king's Exile.

And now, high above us, jutting from the ramparts,
the suddenly changed geography,
The Presidential View Estates
bent all in a row, look down,
for sale.

7. Can You See Viet Nam In My Body?

Rifle raised, green fatigues, running hard
toward us. Angry, his eyes, Oriental, his gun, who? Viet
Cong. He shoves through the window
INSTRUCTIONS FOR VISITORS: NO FOOD ALLOWED IN CAMP.
He shoves us into
twelve years of newsphotos.

Tents. Immigrants. In military order, all in a row, miles
up the wide, dry river bed, dead of summer where it never
rains, California, miles into Ramona,
these people who wrenched me out of Ramona, who wrenched
all of us, refugees now in our own country.
17000. 16 cots to a tent, leg room only between the cots
of strangers, now the only family you got. Dust
rising from our wheels down through tent rows, children
playing football, marines instructing. I look back
into a dark cave, empty but for a baby
in a hammock
rocked back and forth by a long, thin, girl arm.

We pull onto a bluff overlooking Camp 8,
park beneath a tall wooden cross.
Site of First Christian Baptism, Alta, California.
Two teenage couples, each holding hands, sit beneath the cross.
Smiling at us. Where Europeans
first convinced Californians. Behind them, dark figures
walk in the pale hills with coats on their heads.

They say they get headaches from the sun.
In the panic they left their parasols behind.
They go to the hills a lot. A great release I think
to make love, a lot of tension and worry, they miss
their home and families. When they first came
there were about twelve unwanted pregnancies a week.
Now there is only about one. They come in all day
for their birth control.

A woman's highpitched voice
like Indian women keening for their dead
booms up the arroyo, a strange tongue, a loud
foreign speaker, where Ramona dreams, as air, as song and light.
The teenagers smile at us, the native faces
translucent in the raw land of cowboy movies,
where the Del Mar Fossil was recently found,
of people here 48000 years ago,
and thirty Chinese stone anchors sitting on the bottom of the sea
off Los Angeles, left here a thousand years
before Columbus.

8. Marcelene, in Swiss Accent:

They are materialists.
They believe in their material goods. It is their religion.
They believe all Americans hate the Communists as they do.
Many are second-time refugees, having fled North Viet Nam first in the 50s.
They have chosen twice to keep their money and way of life over Communist ideals.
Most have lots of money, or did: the business men and Army personnel.
Still, there are many peasants who want to return,
who are resentful for being hauled over here.
Some say they were kidnapped, force-panicked into fleeing.
There's a group that claims they were drugged.
Some are going back. They have to go to Guam first.
It is the rainy season there and conditions are very uncomfortable.
They have to wait there a long time, probably a year,
until the Communists have carefully investigated them.
To make sure they aren't spies.

9.

In those tents the English classes are conducted.
In those tents are the survival classes, how to shop in supermarkets.
In those tents in the middle, the Mess---
is that what you call it? funny word for the place to eat---
the Mess Hall. Vietnamese food and cooking
is strictly prohibited, part of the Americanization.
They have to learn to eat hotdogs.
I don't understand the food business. One day
a woman got a chicken and was cooking it Vietnamese style
for everyone in her tent. The Marines smelled it,
came and took it away. Scolded them for breaking the rules.
It must be very hard to be forbidden to eat the food you've always eaten.
One day they went on strike. Dumped their dinners in the garbage.
They complained of cold, bad food. The newspapers
were full of angry letters from taxpayers
outraged at the ingratitude of the refugees.

The Vietnamese are like the French of Europe,
the most arrogant, the high race of the Orient,
the most intellectual and sophisticated.
The Cambodians are like the Portuguese of Europe,
softer, nicer, more submissive. One woman said to me
You know, we Vietnamese are sometimes mean. We are
40% mean and 60% good. And we are more intellectual.

10.

A doctor in Rancho Santa Fe sponsored a chief of police
from one of the cities. Last week they were going to dinner.
The doctor invited me because I speak French.
I spent the evening talking with the police chief's wife.
I was the first person she had been able to talk to
since arriving here. She described over and over
soldiers killing women and babies and each other
for food and places on the boat. She kept saying a child was lost
in the churning wake of their overcrowded boat.

Now you understand, her husband, a chief of police,
would have been killed by the Communists.
And they would have killed his wife. But his wife knows nothing.
Nothing. She is completely naive and innocent.
It was a surprise to her to have to leave her country.
She was never allowed to know that that could happen. Or why.
They were very wealthy but she didn't own a suitcase.
When he came home and told her to pack she found it so impossible
to comprehend, her servants had to pack for her.
She arrived here without any of the things she would have saved or brought.
There really were women who hardly knew a war was going on.

My psychiatrist told me it was probably a mistake
for me to have come to this country
because it has made me too independent for my marriage to work.
I told him the story of this woman, the wife of the police chief
who would have been killed even though she knows nothing
about her country or the war. I told him the men
in the old world

keep their wives innocent and ignorant. I told him
women bring the people into the world.
They must learn to take responsibility for it
rather than continue to be
the lighthearted slightly stupid wife
happy in bed.

11.   Palomar Observatory

Years I couldn't sleep for the bombs
around Ramona everyone claimed they couldn't hear.
Years of driving the coast highway, my little boy
dying to see the war games, naval ships and tanks
landing on the beaches, troops marching into the hills.

Near the unmarked graves of astronomers on Mt. Palomar
we camped with my parents.
My children and I posed for our picture
on the observatory steps as I had posed with them
when I was their child. All night
while the Eye peered into infinity
and we tried for reconciliation
the marines rehearsed
until I came down
crazed with family and war games
to the iodiney sea.
I met a marine with his orders for Nam
who gazed into the sea
and talked of killing,
of being killed.

I can't make sense of the world, he said,
except back there near Ramona.
Sometimes during the games I get away and find myself
alone in one of those arroyos that make you feel
life is good. Then, even on cold nights, a warm current
seems to lift you. If I make it, and I'm sure I won't,
I'm going back into those hills.

The carney air
lifted the pier above the mountains.
The moon came up from the dark Ramona
and I saw the waves
whipping the drowning body
of the only marine I ever loved, his tongue
circling deep beyond the roof of my mouth at fifteen,
fighting the black water for hours, then lost
in the midnight riptide.

12.   Sleeping With The Enemy/ I Don't Want To Talk About It

Like the legless, the armless, the sightless

it gets hard core

I mean, I don't want to talk about it, I mean
Mai Lai, was that it? I mean
level everyone, I mean

little kids come up to you
real sweet, you gotta kill them first
they might have bombs in their shirts

It gets hard core

You push the gooks out
at 500 feet
whether they talk or not

It's a bad thing to write about
It's a bad thing, you shouldn't do it,
you know, make it
marketable

like the legless, the armless, the sightless

I'm not going to say another word
about it, because, of course,
you follow orders

like killing everyone who wears glasses
because it means
they think

like my mad sergeant
who played Mozart every night
so the enemy would know
our location, he loved
the game

like shooting him in the back
when he and I
were the only survivors

like the first person I killed
a pregnant girl
I shot her in the belly
the foetus flew in my face
I've hated women ever since

it's a bad thing to write about

it gets hard core

like prostitutes who jammed
hair pins
into the ears of sleeping boys

like the boys who jammed
grenades
up the cunts
of the village girls

like frontier soldiers who scalped
the genitals of Indian women

and stretched them over saddle-bows
and stretched them over cavalry hats
while riding in the ranks

like being a girl in America
and watching the boy next door
leave for war

like the princess in the fairy tale
it gets hard core, you're
the property, the prize
your father the King gives away
to the warrior
who wins

like war and sex
like men and women
in our Kingdom, follow
the same order, domination
and submission, like war
over the land, like war
over the women,
the spoils, the prize, what's
taken

Like the 4000 member
CIA Killer Squad
Like plastic pellet bombs
that cannot penetrate
steel or rubber, only
human flesh, geared
to explode
at the height of the average Vietnamese

war is about our sex, war is the hatred
of the body, like

napalm, the fleshfire
that can't be put out

like a bomb called the Cheeseburger
like a bomb called the nosebomb

like shooting your sergeant in the back

like CS gas:
you vomit to death

like weather modification

like the armless, the legless, the sightless
you
don't want to talk about it

Like the 22 year old woman
you force water down
then jump on her belly, you, the whole
squadron. You capture her 3 times.
3 times she escapes. Rests.
Comes back to the front, now

her misshapen body, her heels
you shaved off, the finger you plucked.
The color of her skin
is not a color. But you
are in her body now,
the fits she has
wherever she goes, what
you did to her
she repeats over and over
what you don't want to remember

You can do anything to me.
I'll never talk. Free
my country

like the legless, the armless, the sightless

like the bones of 4000 years of Vietnamese
who nourish the rice paddies
like the whole country
a sacred burial ground.

13.   American Citizen

           a.

The language drops in dirt, buried speech, seeds
for sage and lupine

The skin cracks, you leave its colors behind
The uterus fills with politics, and dry
treeless hills that can, someday, yes, be you
but never yours

The face leaks into sun, forgets
the hills that pulled it
this way and that

Your tongue's at a loss, begins to swell
In deepest sleep you hear on old conversation
the skin thinking
what you did to get here
stories in each cell about to
birth, what you saw
through your mother's flesh

How you have changed. The hunger you felt
you have become

Now the earth never returns
to that place
that dreamed you

           b.

All Americans begin with loss
a nervous ache, an act of
treason

We don't love our land
because we're the ones
who always left our land

for some notion of it

PART II: HARD NOW AGAINST THE MAN: FEMALE PROBLEMS

The American part of the war had begun in Danang with mixed and missed signals. Strapping U.S. Marines had marched ashore straight into the arms of school girls in white dresses carrying garlands of flowers. Vietnam opened itself to seduction and a brief, unhappy affair, but America came for rape. A seduction might have ended quietly, with only dissatisfaction. A rape, once began,had to be carried to its conclusion.

1.   The Family Planning Clinic

a.   Sometimes I Understand The Hatred Against Women
You are in conference.
You are planning the war.

I stand in the doorway.
I wait for the appropriate moment,
the moment of woman.

Then I bring you
my tray
of bread and meat.

You kill. And I always
look back into your body.
My mirror.

You lie dead in the street.
I stretch the full length of my body
onto you. I am crying

Let me couple with you still
Let me couple with you still

And the children I bring forth:

I issue to you
and the battlefield.

b.
This place was made for the measure of lovers, Hiroshima
You were made for the measure of my body, Mon Amor

Looking down the long passage into this new country,
the peeling green paint of institutional walls
where the pregnant women sit
on the long wooden bench.

A baby falling down the long passage
into the bloodstained hands of the world
into this new country. The fall
of your country, the fall of your uterus,
this falling down barracks, the fall
of your high round breasts
for his seed.

43

The Vietnamese believe themselves to be
the most beautiful race in the world,
their country the most beautiful country in the world

the high round asses, the amazing faces, *America*
he says, *was seduced by the Vietnamese, that is why*
we stayed so long, to fuck these women

       c.
Some of the peasants are delighted to hear
they can make love and not make a baby every time.
They bring their husbands with them
because they can usually speak French.
Please explain to your wife, I say to him.
She's been popping out babies from her body
while he's been out in the world learning languages.
They look at the box containing all the devices
and they usually choose the Pill.
They look at the pills like they're jewelry
and they don't ask the questions we've learned to ask
about what they do to the body.

          Devour me, destroy me
          Deform me in the manner of your likeness

      d.
In the old days everytime a woman fucked
she took death into her vagina. Death
as in childbirth. Death. Not the fanciful death
of amorous don Juans, not the war games
of young and old men, but death, real, sunk into her
cunt

      if I fuck him it may kill me

and still it is so
so many reasons women withdraw
the odds the same, this century
has simply shuffled them. Now death
as in contraceptives, now death
as in the 8th house, now death
as in sex and death

          Devour me, destroy me
          Deform me that I might perform successfully
          in the streets of the world

e.

Oriental.   Old Woman.   Oriental.   Young one.
Foetus, American. Grandmother, pregnant,
you come down the long hallway, wearing black pajamas
holding yourself the way girls do
who have to pee. You hold the baby in
your falling down uterus, you hold the old skin
from ripping beneath the weight.
You hold the water in against a sinking vessel
come all the way across the seas. His seed, yours,
streaming bloody down the long passage.

f.

I no longer remember his hands that lifted me
but I remember the pain
I no longer remember the force that hit me
but I remember the rain of his body shooting me

How could the world forget and go on living?
I was 20 when Hiroshima was bombed.
Everyone rejoiced. I'll never forget that.
My dead lover was an enemy of my country.

I've been an actress ever since. I will keep acting.
I am a woman, I know everything, therefore
I can do nothing. I can only pretend to live.

g.   The Priest Is Telling Her Story

Coming down from the Northern Highlands, she had the baby on the trail.
Her six children helped her. When the invasion began
they found the husband and managed to get on a barge.
But as they set forth ropes were cut and the man
was on the other barge disappearing in the direction of Saigon
while they sailed for Guam.
They've been here two months. His fate has been unknown
until yesterday when he arrived in this country.
They are here now to be reunited with him, *father,*
husband, provider.

Everyone is happy for the reunion, nurses, marines, the jolly Irish priest
who keeps saying *Only in America* and *You can thank America for this,*
When he gives his license plate letters for his pass,
he informs us all
That's Latin for God Bless America!

Everyone is happy for the reunion
except the woman who is frowning,
Everyone except the wife
whom no one sees

But if you look at her you see
she has prayed
never to see her husband again.

h.
Devour me, destroy me
Deform me in the manner of your likeness
so that no one will ever forget
this depravity
that holds us as one

i.   The Labor
In the midst of international idiocy the body
rages for recognition

We had a woman in here this morning, cancer of the cervix.
We are trying to figure now
what to do with her.

j.
When you enter me you fill my passage with an unearthly light
and I see 200,000 dead in 10 seconds

You are good for me
You destroy me
You make me as one with them

k.
"28" did not make her appointment.
The priests have been telling them
abortion is a sin. Twenty-eight
changed her mind.

l.
The body will record the events and the child
will look like
what happened

He's the psychiatrist here, former Minister
of Health and Welfare in Viet Nam.
He's planning a large study
on the phenomenon of refugees.
What this will do to them.

m.
Now that they are learning English
the orphans flown here in the Spring
claim they are not orphans. They have parents
and want to find them.

A child loses its language in six months
if it doesn't hear it.

You are good for me
You destroy me

n.
A four year old boy machine gunning a marine
who dies, laughing

46

Two boys sneaking up on a woman who wears red high heels,
holds six boxes of birth control pills in her lap

and a boy with a cowboy holster and gun
made for him of folded paper
shooting a blond Vietnamese girl
up and down the green room, falling, rolling, dying

> *Devour me, destroy me*
> *Make me as one with you*

o.   The-Hue, Midwife

The means *girl* and *Hue* means *lily, like the flower.*
Hue displays the jade of the family fortune.
She wears jade in her ears, around her neck,
on each finger, on both wrists, on both ankles.
She wears jade in her silver hair and pinned to her nurse's uniform.
The rest of the family fortune, she explains,
is in a box back in the tent
guarded 24 hours a day
by rotating members of the family.

> *And there is the town of Hue*
> *the town in which General Troung was loved.*
> *He was said to drink cognac late into every evening,*
> *pouring over maps and plans for coming battle.*
> *During the 1968 Tet Offensive he left his wife and family,*
> *jumped into his jeep and shot his way through Vietcong lines*
> *to take command of his men at the front.*
> *Many times there was talk of his removal*
> *and he would go to Hue and walk along the banks of the Perfume River*
> *so the people would know he had not left.*

A midwife for 25 years, I never marry.
But I have 10 year old daughter.
One day I visit Catholic orphanage.
I see ants crawl from ears of deaf and dumb girl.
Ants, you understand, mean life.
I took her to Saigon, treated her
for infection. She was cured.
But when I returned her to orphanage
the nuns say, you must keep her.
Even though you are Buddhist
it is meant by God that you keep her.

Now she thirteen, still slow by the ants, maybe retarded.
But I fix that. I give her age as ten
when we enter this new country!

> *And there was the town of Hueneme*
> *from which the Buddhist monks proceeded*
> *south along the coast*
> *to the basin where tar boils*

My second time in this country. First time, Brooklyn, '71.
For training at abortion clinic. I must tell you
new phenomenon seen everywhere.
Faulty dilation of cervix by abortionists
causing women to lose babies they later want to carry.
At about 5 months. Cervix scarred open. Foetus
fall out. And *Saline Method*

she blurts out suddenly as if in appeal

terrible. terrible. For fifth, sixth month.
Amniotic fluid is withdrawn by large needle
and saline mixture injected. Foetus
struggle like a fish. It turn over. Awful.
Awful.

> *Devour me, destroy me*
> *Make me as one with your race.*

p. Anh
The girl is pregnant,
but her boyfriend went back to Viet Nam.
She is depressed.
She thinks she has a sponsor in Washington D.C.
She wants to go to nursing school.
She was a nurse in Viet Nam. A Jehovah's Witness.
She is thirty-two and wants an abortion.
But I can't talk her into birth control.
She says over and over, *I am thirty-two. I know myself.*
I will not be seduced by a man again.
I will get married in seven years.
But now I don't need birth control.
I don't want it. I won't have it.
I won't be seduced by a man again.

Hue says

She is hard now against the man. She forgets
winter will pass and spring will come and she will be happy again.
She forgets the vision changes.

q.
> *My home is a place I never go back to*
> *but a place I go back to in dreams every night.*
> *I had my first lover there, an enemy of your country.*
> *They shaved my head for loving him, and locked me in a basement.*
> *I went mad. I'm supposed to have died there.*
>
> *Now every night I set my town on fire*
> *and every night the memory of him*
> *sets my body on fire.*
>
> *We were so young when it happened.*
> *My home, Viet Nam. Hiroshima, mon amor.*

r.
When the Cambodians come down from Camp 9,
the child with them will be Black. American.

Both your father and your mother
come down with you. Understand?

Devour me, destroy me

s. Thao
Drifting for days in a small sampan with little water or food.
So many trying to escape it was dangerous to stay close to shore.
We met many ships but none would take us. Afraid we are communists.
At night we came close to shore and anchored.
The first night my mother went home to get something I don't know.
At the last moment my husband made us leave. She had not time to return.
After the third day the owner of the sampan decided to try no more.
He would rather take his chances with the communists.
But they would kill my husband for sure.
On the fifth day two boats came after us flying the Viet Cong flag.
But when they got out to sea near us they threw out the flags.
That must have been their way of escaping the communists.
We are very glad for our escape to freedom.
But my heart hurts for my mother.

Deform me in the manner of your likeness.

t.   The Mysteries
Across the wall the western script of Viet Nam.
Down the wall the ideogrammatic script of Cambodia.
In any language, how to make love
and not make a baby
KE HOACH ROA DIA DINH
TU CUNG

but if you do, if something goes wrong
if you can't help yourself
if it's not a sin
if your boyfriend goes back
if your mother and father come down with you

the five methods then
of abortion

      Endometrial Aspiration
      Dilation and Curettage
      Aspiration and Curettage
      Hysterectomy
      The Saline Method

KE HOACH ROA GIA DINH
TU CUNG

      vagina, uterus, fallopian, penis, semen, baby
      in any language

Tu cung means vagina, Hue says.
Do you think *tu cung*
is the sailor's origin
of cunt?

and over the illustration for vasectomy
in four languages she has written
in a large urgent hand

VASECTOMY IS NOT CASTRATION!

They make appointments for it and never return.
The priests are telling them
they won't be able to come anymore.

> *You are good for me.*
> *You make me as one with them.*

> u.
> *When you enter me it is as passage all through the city*
> *I see the anonymous hair falling*
> *from a woman while she sleeps*
>
> *You are good for me, you blind me.*
> *The principle of inequality had stranded me.*
> *How could I not be one of them?*
> *But now, at last, you destroy me.*

> v. Ramona
come closer, shed softly
your watery eyes. She stands in the glassy sun
at the end of the hall: her
dark silhouette. She leans against
the door looking in.
Coat on her head.

Your hair is beautiful, she says to me
touching it.
So blondness. Marilyn
Monroe.

> *Prepped, I'm rolled through the green hall*
> *to abort our child.*
> *You walk out*
> *because I'm crying.*
> *The nurses see me. These Mendocino Portuguese women,*
> *wives to fishermen, loggers.*
> *They whisk me into a side room, whisper*
> *so the doctor can't hear*
>
> *You don't have to do it.*
> *You could change your mind.*

w.
Examine the nation, stranded in her cunt,
her cunt to clutch you, castrate you.
Come in, she'll open, she'll take you in.

The doors open. See
the unborn stranded, the heart
without a country.

The doctor is saying
She's had no periods since May
but she doesn't feel pregnant.
She's firm.

In May they came down the Long Trail.
The refugee coming from the north
came into your city, recorded the events
in your body. You fucked so hard
you wanted to climb back into her.

She had jewelry   she had gold
She hardly knew a war was going on

     x. French Pastry
Rings on her fingers, diamonds in her hair,
rhinestones, scowls, bows on her toes,
she shall have things
wherever she goes.

He comes running to share the Paris magazine with her, photos
of the invasion, a man dead in the street.
His voice lifts. She shows no emotion.
She wears gold on her ankles. She has jewelry.

He sees me watching, moves to my bench.
*I was lieutenant-colonel in South Vietnamese Army, Chief
of Troop Transportation.* He shows me
pictures of the dead man. *My friend, my very good
friend. The Saigon Chief of Police.*

This is my Main Street.
He looks at me
as if I do not understand. *You understand
I saw the VC flag
flying over the Presidential Palace.
My poor friend here
saw the tanks.*

A deep river cuts down his eyes
to mountains. High
cheekbones.

I understand
the Thirty of April. Even the Americans
didn't want you.

I understand jailor, underground cages, phoenix murderer, the maimed
and tortured drowning in the river trenches of your face

I understand the Thirty of April.
I was walking in Sacramento.
The Symbionese Liberation Army was leaving Sacramento.
In the window of a tiny Chinese Cafe I saw the headlines
The Communist take over: SAIGON RENAMED HO CHI MINH CITY.
I was understanding as I walked around and around the Capitol
I am pregnant. Invaded. What I must go through now.
I thought then of women
pregnant in a revolution.
unable to abort.

My wife, he boasts, *was owner of French Pastry shop.*

And I understand your wife.
She must have lipstick to help her forget.
She will spill sugar wherever she goes.
She shall change
from one dress to another
in search of her skin

where the child
is being thrown daily
into the churning wake
of our overloaded boat.

      y.   Hue
I will tell you of Vietnamese music

> *A long time ago when things were different*
> *the King had over 100 wives.*
> *One woman was 18 and very beautiful.*
> *She was intellectual and she wrote*
> *how-do-you-say-it? Poesy.*
> *She was chosen by the King to be his wife.*
> *She went to his palace to live, to wait*
> *for the time he would call her.*
>
> *But her whole life passed*
> *because the King was too busy*
> *passing the time to his other wives*
> *to get around to her. She wrote*
> *and wrote, mourning that she was never*
> *visited by the King. Her whole life*
> *passed by her.*

Now the times have changed. Now she climb
over the wall and gets new husband!

Hue begins to laugh, a green tumble and whirl,
her jade body doubling to the floor.
And Anh behind her, who sits so darkly in the window
looking down on the camp, who knows herself
but forgets the seasons change,
begins laughing.
And Marcelene and my sister, Donna, begin laughing.
Soon we are all laughing, a long green room
of pregnant women laughing,
women who are here to jump the wall, laughing,
women who have already jumped the wall
laughing so that we can't stop laughing, women
rolling in the aisle roaring

how the times have changed, a whole people
have jumped the wall!

z.

She took you in, took you deep within,
the man who could make her do anything

Fuck me on the marriage bed,
put me on the birth bed,
I shall dream the deathbed.
Make me one with your race, your face
intent on falling on me.
Deform me in your likeness,
make me one with this place.

I am a woman. I am immoral. I like men.
I sleep with many of them.
When I hold myself apart from them
I hold myself in sin.

Flood me, deflower me, pollute me, blind me.
Make me as my city, the 200,000 dead.
You are a man. You know nothing. Therefore you can do
anything.

2.   Main Street
Back through the tents, dust rising, past old adobe walls,
the original rancho, where now the General lives.
Refugees. Struggle like a fish out of water. Refugees.
Aborted. Fighting the dark waters against a midnight riptide,
in your mouth his tongue, in your body forever.
Cervix scarred open. You have jewelry
you have gold. What he'll do
to get it.

Now Ramona drifts over the boulders, over the bare mountain range
in the appalling light, now softened by ocean breeze

Past his San Clemente exile, the Presidential Palace,
down the King's Highway
over the Mexicans still bent
in a row

Now Ramon, Mojave long dead in an unmarked soldier's grave
pulls me down in fields. I see his face
for the first time, the summer behind him.
The clouds float like rivers through this black hair.
The sun now stone. Golden foxtails
rattle above us

and he rose with her   unwounded
to the thin virgin air. Run!
Take his seed and
Run!

Take the oldest child by the hand.
Sling the other on your back.
Run this path, now run down this one. Teach them
to run. Don't look back.
You are a woman
a violation
to your country.

Run like you know where you are going. (You do.
Run like your home is in the next village
and then in the village beyond that. (It is.
Run. With your eyes straight ahead.
Hide. These bushes. This rock. Tell them they can't
cry.

Leave. Do not believe. Run west. Run against the
war. Hold your life by journeys.
Run through the yellow trees toward the rain.
Follow the sun.
You are a woman.
No nation
recognizes you.

You can leave. (They won't notice.
Climb the river bank, the mountain slope.
Cross the border.
You can arrive. (They won't see you.
You are a woman. You are free.
Run through the cities.
This is your Main Street.
Run to the sea.
Walk over the waters.
Go to another country.
Any country. Run
against the man's war.
Do not believe him.
He wants your children.
Run for their lives.

You are a mother.
They want your son
to murder.

You are a mother.
They want your daughter
for spoils.

(Do not believe
a mother ever
gave her child
to war.
Remember
birth.

You are a woman a danger.
They fear you more than
armies.

You are a woman. Now in this late century
it is time to act
like a woman.
Leave. Take your children away
from war. Teach them to run
from all government. Scatter them
among men and women as you go.

You are a woman.
Your eyes run back and forth
through the whole earth.

You see
beyond all
borders.

Part II
HEADLAND

HEADLAND, I
RAMON/RAMONA

I Was Born Coming To The Sea

I was born in Seaside Hospital on a Long Beach.
The buoy I heard calling from the sea
was a boy calling me
a year to the day they left Ducktown, Tennessee.
While I was coming, Daddy rode the rails
to catch the wheat harvest in Washington,
Mama waitressed the last road west,
a Japanese cafe at the end of Redondo Beach pier.
We rode the Midnight Ghost, Daddy and I gone north for some money,
while Mama and I at the sunset end of the world
brought food from across the sea.

Mama walked all day the hilly streets
above the long sea the day I was born,
the new city risen from the earthquake of '38.
The buoy I heard calling was a sailor who cried
from Japanese war, *don't bring a child
into this world*, everyone told them.
But they laughed. Mama was an orphan.
I felt her hold me as her mother had held her
through the orphanage walls. All my life
I've heard them laughing in the dark,
the sea lapping at the doors,
the gulls flapping in the windows,
the boy calling through the storm.

Thanksgivings we were too poor for turkey.
I pointed to a seagull, said my first sentence.
That's okay, Mama, Daddy can shoot an ea-gull.
When the ships came in from war, Friday nights,
payday when there was work, we went down to the Pike,
ate shrimp from Shrimpy Joe's, so cheap we bought bagfulls.
We watched the boys come home to neon,
to toothless, grinning, redlipped women who tattooed
Mother on their chests.
Then we drove out the shaky night docks of Terminal Island,
sat on the foggy edge beneath groaning oil wells
and the dark squeaky hulls of returned battleships.
They told me the sound was a boy out there
telling boats how to come in through the fog.
I listened to the waves slapping him around.
I heard his crying, his lonely orphanage in the sea.
When we fished, I cast my line to him, I was coming
to the sea when I was born,
the buoy I heard through water and storm
was a boy calling me.

Father

I am like you, Mama always said.
Often we went fishing.
It takes patience and silence
to be a fisherman.
Most fail, you always said.

I am like you, Mama always said,
and if I reach back far enough
we are fishing again from the narrow rock ledge
that jettied the ocean at Seal Beach.
We crawled out to where crabs and unnameables crawled
out of dark seaweedy crevices, the dark holes
the ocean kept screaming up from.
We sat there, always on the dark side, for hours.
days.

It takes patience and silence
to be a fisherman.
We sat in the cold, cruel spray
of wave after wave churning to shore,
and with the contorted fishy bodies
of fishermen, old, toothless, bearded,
their awful cries above the cries of gulls
after deserted mussel.
bait.

I am like you, Daddy, Mama always said.
Your body a great melancholy night in which I sat
beneath your heart
in terrible silence
and fished.

The old men danced as the day
moved on, those
fishers, those broken
bearded kings, those
Ahabs.
As the flaming ball fell
to the water line between my thighs
I was a drowned creature
drifting hundreds of years
in the unspeakable
foundations.

Unwarped, unarguable shapes
glided to and fro
before my passive eyes.
Did I ever catch a fish?
Did I ever want to?

I wanted only
to sit there longer
on the dry landside of my father
knowing the shadow of my father is my father.
Daddy, still I wake
on that broken throne of gnarled torsos.
Daddy, the dark power you cast
I took.

Though sometimes still
the girl curls
into your humped darkness,
contorts her fishy body
into the great heartsea
beneath your ribs

and in silence
works her way all the way back
to an old woman coming from Asia
and further than that
to an old white whale
cruising the pelvis of the world

until our story (You, the ruthless boy
so young even still
I see you outlive me)
is turning into
foam
and the great birth
from your severed and flung
genital.

Charon

When I was a child I couldn't sleep.
In a small stucco house south of Los Angeles
I learned my family by night,
their bodies through the house
like dark mansions into which we were drifting
my eyes so wide open
the night was that whole basin of immigrants
migrating before me

On our vacations
we started out in early evening,
the car draped in canvas waterbags,
and drove east all night across the desert
to avoid the heat of the day.
My father drove, the others slept.
I sat behind his silent body
awake in the cross blast of four open windows,
the wind burning, like sand from mesas,
the flesh from my face, and any words
back down my throat. We never talked
as we sped across the empty floors, the Mojave,
the Salton Sea, the Colorado, Death Valley,
my father and I the only creatures in the world
awake

except at the neon-lit truck stops
where the diesels hummed
and the laughter carried
miles out into the waste, and *her* voice
tough, sexy, bringing food

so that for the rest of my life
I would think my occupation
must naturally be
waitress

helping night travelers
to get across
before the light comes up

Santana

In this last moment, I burst into childhood.
The hot buzzard wind pulls me to the secret.
My legs pound down the bluelit basin, my lungs call
the blond L.A. sky

and I am any girl they run
down the cyclone fence that saves us
from the Los Angeles River, further and further back
to the sand dunes where no one ever plays,
powerful in the leap of tumbleweeds,
magnificently chased by the 6th grade boys.
I'm the fastest kid in the school,
the anchor man on the relay team,
but now, like any girl, they gain on me,
as effortlessly we fly, we churn down the porous earth,
we pour through the clouds, we shout over the river's roar
of boulders crashing down the San Gabriels
flooding our long, concrete ditch
where wetbacks and cowboy stars
ride the west out of time and sometimes, as now
in the last spring of elementary school, water,
sweeping the mutilated, the murdered,
the awashed in wind and light,
to sea.

The stormfence catches me. Caged. I turn.
In the blinding light they fly at me,
hummingbirds! the dark feathered streaks
and whirring beaks no higher
than my adult breasts.

One reaches to touch me.
An electric spark rents the air.
The blue of their mouths open, their faces lift
to the Face of the fathers.
I see my own face far below
on the river bank, a hobo hurrying south.
Suddenly I know why I've never played.

When I walk away, the light
shatters the holy body behind me,
so many feathers to the Witches' Wind.

L.A. Blonde

(For barry eisenberg who, on finding a photograph of me at sixteen as a
beauty queen parading down Main Street on the hood of a baby blue Thunder-
bird, said, *"God, Sharon, you have a lot of karma to work out."*)

Something of the light on sage there,
the light exploding off the ocean.
Something of the burning light pouring onto the hills,
hurling back down the canyons as flame.
And the beautiful stars running into the light,
and the beautiful stars running out of the light
from reeling earthquake, live oak,
and the rampage of ice plant.

Shadow and light
of the groundswells, the highways and beaches
washed clean by Santana, hot
Grandmother of God and hard rains
in an hour, the danger then
in the dry beds of flash flood,
the swollen arroyos
that undermine every house in the foothills.
The danger then of the city
pushing you off
into the unwatered desert.

The way on winter days
it's almost light enough
to photograph something like
angels in the Eucalyptus, the one hundred
varieties, and hummingbirds,
symbol of resurrection, hovering
the cacti gardens.
And high over the bird of paradise,
palm and poinsettia,
vulture
that only light has blinded
to the secret
of bougainvillaea.

Marilyn Monroe said she was always running into
other people's unconsciouses.
You lift the hand from the pale ice of your gown
to the dark electricity of air.
The sun heats the hood, turns your shoulders red.
You wave along the collective stare lining the boulevard.
In the blinding light they appear
like a negative risen from solution,
the skin black,
the eyes, hair, teeth, and nails,
as they roar, *Blondie!*
bleached out.

Ramon/Ramona

There are your wars, deadly-winged wildcats
crawling the sky, Korean Migs and B52s
firebombing trapped soldiers on the ground.

You draw these battles
in every class, on any paper or book
while the teacher drones on
and the sweaty fat woman who is actually only 17,
whose name is whispered among us in the showers
and hissed by you when we hide in the hills
to curse the town, paints, at her easel,
unceasingly, oils.

A red wave blown by Santana Wind across the desert
laps the mountain from Julian
and pours toward us. Enormous ashes
fall like snow, like autumn leaves
blackening the valley. At Inaja
a box canyon sucks in fire.
Seventeen firefighters, fame of your Mojave,
are gone.

I paint Monterey Cypresses I have never seen
dreaming of the lives of water.
Weeks ago I first showed you my breasts.
Now at night you come from your hide-out in the hills,
climb the pepper tree to my window.
My sister sleeps in the small room.
I pull the blanket over us
to muffle the cries, your fiery breath
sucking me to a box canyon.
We struggle from rocks,
to the unexpected soft hills of flesh.
But I don't let you enter me.

I watch you make a fist
around the pencil, stab and tear the paper
to kill the man whose arms are raised
holy and helpless on the ground.
I can't help but look to the forked levi place
of the boys seated around me,
though it is their hands
that shock me, to think
of the secret places they have found,
the secret things they can do.

And the girl who is already old
who left school long ago
and returns now to this one all-day class
paints a thick, redlipped woman
whose blouse is pulled from the shoulder
whose Indian skirt is full of painted words:
Mexican Madonna, Mona Lisa, Venus and Mars.

Even now I do not understand
her terrible name, a hellplace full of fire and hate.
A deadend canyon of charred bodies
feared even by Santana,
war, dust and stone.

Hall of Justice: The Sixties

1.
Before they brought you home
I walked my childhood hill in Ramona
in search of sage to send you.
When I cut the brush it opened
and I saw the dirtwomen
grinding acorn in heavy air
that roared and beat, then shifted
my monotonous body.

2.
In that state even on the outside
such smells were dead.
That was your first cold winter.
That was the winter the snow
filled the Grand Canyon.
That was the jail
you touched yourself
only twice in the year
so quick was the light
the guard's triumphant yell
exploding over the blanket
you were to keep warm beneath.

3.
L.A. wanted you more.
They brought you home
for Christmas.
In the parking lot
I danced over the sun
that burned in broken glass
for someone who looked down
from the 13th floor
and over the winter Birds
of Paradise.

4.
I rose through granite
with large mothers from Watts
who cried when the door opened
to their sons caught
in the green cage.

And you would enter
like a pale virgin among them,
untouchable behind glass, and ground
like a mother to her knees.

Ramon, My Country Tis of Thee

In her hair the moon weaves the town.
From down out of the mountains he comes,
the man outside.
As he walks down into the town
the moon pulls its cold light across his face,
a miner's face, a mime's face

Curious, she follows him down Main Street
always ten feet or so behind, always watching.
She sees that the others on the street don't see him.
She sees his face ahead of him
in the slanted display glass of the stores,
a young boy dressed in ragged, filthy miner's clothes
as if he has come a hundred years
from the goldrush town in the mountains
from Julian down to Ramona
to buy his supplies or stake his claim
or just to look around
because he's been gone a hundred years
and that's why he looks so surprised, but also
sorrowful

Through his long hair she sees the country being settled
and then she sees herself in the window
following behind him

For the rest of her life she will not know
where he went or why the others did not see him
or why even
he takes no notice of his own image
or of hers

and so She travels him
She, the Voyeuristic Lover
the Witness
Her body hears the earth

and He travels her
history
with its pure light on the record
of the real meeting

and through the glass the country is being settled
The moon pulls its cold light over.
their home, a covered wagon
covering the country
and all nations

travel them

Ramona, 1956-
Albion, 1976

70

HEADLAND, II
BICENTENNIAL

Truly buzzards
Around my sky are circling!

For my soul festers
And an odor of corruption
Betrays me to disaster

Meanness, betrayal, and spite
Come flockwise
To make me aware
Of sickness and death within me.
My sky is full of the dreadful sound
Of wings of unsuccesses.

Washoe-Paiute
tr., Mary Austin, 1904

His mind is too simple, I cannot go on
sharing his nightmares

My own are becoming clearer, they open
into prehistory

which looks like a village lit with blood
where all the fathers are crying: My son is mine!

Adrienne Rich

The Dream

In a large city draped in the flags of sorrow,
I separate from my love.
I search for him through many cities
and across the seas.
Through Europe I travel by train.

Along roads torn into interstates
and through the construction shells for new houses
I look for him.
I look for him in a redwood forest still virgin
and along the edge of a Mendocino road still dirt.

The sky is silver water
and I am in a car with him.
Streamers and tincans fly from the sides
in celebration of the wedding.
But behind us, in the trailer that we pull
my sister hovers and cries.
I try to quiet her
but she weeps through everything.

Three brides come down the street.
Our veils are thick and long,
our arms are interlocked.
But as we enter the church
we let each other go
to secure the masks across our faces.

I look back to the dark whiskey bar
at the rear of the church.
Ramon is sitting there.
All this time he's been hiding
on the Reservation at Santa Ysabel.

I run to meet him, slipping beneath
the legs of the guests,
crawling beneath the pews.
He looks beautiful
even though he was killed
many years ago when his car
leaving Ramona, hit a Eucalyptus tree
on Highway 67.
Now we huddle together
whisper, celebrate
in the dark, church bar.

Now I'm writing letters to him.
I'm waiting for him to return.
I'm writing of our separation.
I'm writing of Viet Nam.

Then in slow, lucid motion
the spinning, streaming, exploding car
shatters him into Eucalyptus.
Repeated and repeated
as he steps on a mine,
as he's shot from the ambush,
as he's pushed from the copter

and the face of the girl
seen in the car
and the face of the girl
seen below on the ground

I lay myself down on her and plead

let me couple with you still

Psyche In January

1. Emanuelle

You spend your holidays
trying to write a poem
of the pornographic film
Emanuelle.

The Lord himself shall give you a sign:
a virgin shall conceive and bear a son
and they shall call his name Emanuel
which means God is with us. *As noun*
the Messiah.

As you come from the dark theater
sorting the welter of seductive images,
Loretta says

At last I understand the connection
between romance and pornography.

You spend your January trying to write a poem
based on a rejection from the Massachusett's Review
and if you think you are redeemed by love
or anything else
you are a fool

a poem in which the connection,
erotic and true, of this film
is Christmas, your country.

2. Lilith

But only the night knows you.
On the air over Albion Ridge

Lily...   Lily...   Lily...

a woman in your hometown, *los angeles*
goes on trial for the murder of another

She cut the woman's throat
then cut the baby out.
She took it to the hospital
claimed she had just given birth.

3. Waitress

On the 9th you wake from hard labor.
In the moon's jeering shaft
you try again
to see his sleeping face.

Not even the night knows:
I wanted you to lock the doors
lie down on the tavern floor
let them all fuck you.

But this morning as you were leaving
I strangled you,
snuffed you out forever
for doing what you did
in my fantasy.

4. Cinderella
On the 11th
you wake beneath redwood

We must kill her
the veterinarian said,
her heart is too large.

As the sun went down you lay her
in her shining black coat
under the cathedral round of redwood
that grows behind your cabin.

You buried all your strange secrets, 14
years, married her to death, at last
to her name
Cinder
to the legendary ash
in red clay, to the prince
of trees.

5. Isis
On the 15th the night finds you
hunting through the town's festive streets
hoping an accidental meeting
will bring you together

fate,   rather than
crass design

Instead, it will be an accidental parting,
meeting him in the morning
after you've been told
he's already gone.

He has one foot
on the boat deck
and one on the land.
The sweet flesh of his chest
beneath the unbuttoned shirt
aches untouched
in your opened hand.

You know you have lost him.
The water, as you speak,
laps gently his foot on the manmade platform.
It could not have been different,

ghost, you see all your beloved animals
dead in red clay
and a long row
of hung men.

6. Sappho
On the 18th you take a middle-aged woman home.
She calls the house in Mendocino
her *beautiful castle.*

Her house is grotesque, a mausoleum.
But you are in love with her.
You watch her walk to the door.
You don't understand why her house
is more important than her life.

But when she confided
she is going to shave her head on Wednesday,
the night deepened, you wanted
to make love to her.

You try to turn around.
The street is too narrow.
You find your old car
in the house of strangers.

7. Ramona
All the week of the 20th
armies march across your land,
crazed white men killing your men.
You are conquered with each conquest,
you die
each death.   Only

the night knows you are stranded
at 3 a.m. on the bridge over Big River.

The accident victim is bloody, wandering.
Even beneath the full moon, redwoods that pierce
the rushing nightclouds, he doesn't see
he's blocking traffic.

When you finally get home
he beats you.
You stay silent so the guests
still here from Christmas
and your children
won't hear.
You stay silent because even in this
you are faithful to him.

8. Psyche
Toward the end you see them coming,
a caravan of gypsy trucks
down from Canadian winter.

They camp this night in redwoods.
The relationship of all his lovers is confusing
but there is the beautiful river
flowing through the giant trees, down
into the wide, lush meadows.

And beneath the crimson and black sky
waist-deep in the river
are all the beautiful men.
Ahead of them
are the dangerous falls.

They are so deep
into their stories, into the world's beauty,
you, a voyeuristic lover,
have no place.

You climb the marble steps of the ruins,
to forget,
to lie on your back in peace,
to observe Orion, your blind constellation.

But a man below, on your left,
sees you, begins to climb.

You flee. He chases.
He becomes a mob.
You run through the institution
where you birthed your daughter.
He becomes a giant monster of yourself, *la
llorona, la chingada, rose of sharon,*
the head of a large angry crowd
that intends to kill you.

Inside, you bolt the cathedral door.
You wear a bridal dress and veil.
You hold the door shut against the mob
while your family runs for help.

But the key is turning
from the outside.
You are doomed.

Loretta, your pretty bridesmaid,
stands calmly, ironic witness
beside the door
that opens now

The monster grabs you, she is
you, a huge extinct fur
slithering around her neck, a lit
orange, a bizarre light.

She hands Loretta a detailed sheet of instructions,
your tasks. She takes your arms
and twists them, like braiding rope,
24-36-64 times,
all the way down to your thumbs.

You wake. The bucking light
remains on the wall over your head.
You turn on the lamp
before she wakes him.

The monstrous lit Rose, *Lilith, Lucifer, Emanuel,*
spilt oil, lost shoe, apple, phallus, Marilyn, sister,

is still here.

The Poet's Uncle in February

All afternoon he sits in your kitchen
telling his life
into the recorder your father gave you for Christmas.
His heart is bad.

The cypress in the windows lean away
then spring back to hear his words.
The Pygmy Forest begins to grow, ponderosa
over G Road Lake, to think.

Your aunt, whose face was carved long ago
from these tales, sits carefully
beside his last words.
She touches his wrist, nods to the machine.
Are you sure, honey, you want that *down?*

He wants everything down, the story
only he knows, down saved
as the great body only he knows
cannot be.

The sun slides behind the bullpines.
The sailor's sea, two miles to the west, shouts
and the foghorns in three different dogholes,
Little River, Albion, Navarro,
cry back. A lifer, a navigator,
he tells you what they warn.

Albion Ridge grows dark, cold.
This is a myth that has no dates.
You discover the recorder isn't on.

You are witness then
to one of his deaths.

I can't do it again, he moans.

You promise him

I'll remember,
I'll write it all down.

February 12, 1976

LETTER TO LUKE BREIT IN POINT ARENA

Dear Luke: Yesterday, near dusk, I walked down the ridge
to Albion's post office and store. This time, descending,
the Pacific was a hugh eyeball of water
arched over to Asia: Robinson Jeffers, I think, years ago
living on this same headland, three hundred miles south.
Narcissus and daffodils made passage toward the sun
until it disappeared like *a coin placed in a slot.*
I'm not sure how one keeps the life-sustaining images
of other poets from one's work, the way they enter
the body like sperm to the egg, or why, even, one should strain
after new ones since the old ones are forgotten. Returning,
the heavy groceries and six-hundred foot climb slowing me,
I read a letter from Philip sharing *with you weeping*
the abortion that he and Sarah had that morning in Berkeley.
I climbed through his anguished insistence that the foetus
is revealed in the fat robin in the tree and thought
how important that fathers be present at abortions,
my body beneath coat and sweaters bathing in a fine sweat,
the dark Eye of earth behind me, watching, as the poet knew,
not our wars.

I worked all night. For weeks I've struggled with the history
of this country, to write a few simple poems about it.
At this point, just one line, one image, would seem victorious.
I sleep beneath a map now and know myself
as Williams' pure product of America going crazy,
what I cannot express, the slaughters, and the great broken tongue
of the people. Martin Luther King said a riot
is a language of the people and Philip once said that language
has been used to repress Americans and I've always felt
as Billy Budd, my life at stake on the words
that won't come, mute before the obvious. I worked all night,
my family deep in sleep around me, using pen
in this small cabin so as not to wake them with typing,
reading through the dozen books, wading through stories and flesh,
and dislocation and death, searching for the key
to this overstuffed country, stories and people and land
I have pulled to myself, like sperm to the egg:
the American soul, hard, isolate, stoic, and as Lawrence said:
a killer. Your unanswered letter has sat by my bed
for days now. I kept thinking I would reread it. Somewhere
in this history is love. I worked all night, but at 5:45am
I gave up. Slipping on boots I went outside. Over the redwoods,
in the east, a shaft of light delicately split the night
and within it an even more tremulous sight, a comet
spraying gold, dropping directly behind the rising sun,
a measure it seemed of worlds within worlds,
of passage, of an infinite slot, a great unbroken tongue
telling a story. I thought of Crane's pioneer woman
on the long trail back from the gold mines
encountering a homeless squaw bent westward, riding without rein,
and how in the middle of this doomed and damned continent,
against the long teamline of silent, sullen men
they waved their babies at each other. The sun rose

consuming the comet and me without my poem. I fixed
oatmeal, toast, and orange juice for my children
and when they left listened to the school bus
gearing down the ridge, making stops, vaguely anxious
of the time when I will not fix them breakfast.
I didn't have my poem, not even the one line I had especially sought,
but finally, going to bed, I reached for your letter,
and in the sweet exhaustion of my body, I read you.
And I understood, Luke, that you are the poem, the passage
I had sought all night, the love with which you begin
and the love with which you make
poems for the people, and your faith that there is
a place in each of us that can't sell out, yes, even though
the heart as prisoner. Always, you say, people protest
the gentleness of your poems, so empty of the violence
of your life, the Revolutionary awaiting execution
in a Spanish prison, your dead wife and son in Mexico,
but you continue to insist that the gentleness
is a result of the violence
and necessary to your life. Yes, *the heart as prisoner,*
but the line comes to me now: *to pull dead Indians
from the soil,* and with the heart's love, I enter your poetic form,
always so accessible, take it from you and send it back:
to you, and to the people, through this letter: democracy.
My man woke and loved me, hours it seemed, my body
exploding in the cries of all our babies never to be born,
consuming a solar comet spraying hope across a land
that this year celebrates 100,000 year old Mojave Man,
and the Eye that watches more than our wars.

Visions of A Daughter of Albion
(Eleven Valentines for America, February 14, 1976)

1. Land of Heart's Desire
I sleep beneath a map of this country
and dream she is loving her body
out of political boundaries
I hear her crying
what is this place to me
if you are lost?

Now I sleep beneath America
Sacajawea leading Lewis and Clark across the uncharted world

Prairie grass so high mounted soldiers are lost

Waiting days for mile-wide buffalo herds
to cross in front of you

Now I sleep beneath America
and pull white men from the prohibitive world
deeper into my wilderness
and the promise of sexual love

Cherokees across miles of my flesh
Redwood trees that never die

I am ploughing North America
the night that is our history
the Body we must put our bodies up against

O, but you are dreaming me she cries
because she knows
bloodlines that have been lost
and blood
that has so soaked

the frontier and all the lands left behind
her soul can find
no well of clear water

2.
Your face is strange
And the smell of your garments
But your soul is familiar
As if in dreams our thoughts
had visited one another

Often from unremembering sleep
I wake delicately glowing
Now I know what my heart was doing

Now I know why when we met
It slipped
So easily into loving

Washoe-Paiute Glyph (translated by Mary Austin, 1904)

3.
You send out signals for who and what you need
you told me later.
You stood in my door, uninvited.

I was reading about southern women
singing the Tennessee mining protest song
I Am A Girl Of Constant Sorrow

You will argue with me later
The original song is
I Am A Man Of Constant Sorrow

He has brought you to my door, *a gift.*
I want to tell you both,
priests in Santa Fe took the hearts of Indians
out through their backs, that all over this continent

native women made love
to white men
and believed it good

Show me on the map where you are from
Tell me how I've needed you and you have come
Tell me about Karma, that love brings death

Answer for me Pohatan's question
*Why will you take by force
what you may obtain by love?*

Put your mouth on my heart, lo
body and soul, Whitman said, this land

and its losses, its losses

4.   Psyche
He met the two of you at Albion Market
He saw you do not love her.
You are impressed by his perceptiveness.
Through everything, you will remain
faithful to him, you who also yearn
for your brother.

He saw how pretty you are
there against the great sea,
how I would like you
without you being a threat to him.
He saw that you are tourists, you will leave
never to be seen again.
Coming up Albion Ridge you think he jokes
when he suggests *let's not tell our names.*

Now they love in the loft,
whispers and moans, little laughs
in our daughter's bed.
You say to me
*Women understand everything
and therefore can do nothing.
Men understand nothing
and therefore can do anything.*

They descend the loft.
He stokes the fire.
Only in one context
does he acknowledge spirit,
the spirit's desertion of the flesh
after sex.

The rain whacks the cabin.
We eat bread I have kneaded.
I tell you I'm a poet.
I see my words go into your flesh
like seed to soil
and begin to grow
a new story
which will cause him to flee.

In bed he whispers
amused, amazed,
*When I got inside her
she was disappointing.
It was no different
than being inside you*

and it all comes undone,
the years falling like my father's playing cards
of naked women posed
in dated fashion.

I am a woman who understands everything
including, now, this.
From now on
I will act.
From now on
he must understand.

He must love me
as much as I love him.

I look across the cabin to her,
burnished goddess in the lamp,
silent sister, and inside,
just like me,
a disappointment.

When you leave
when this long weekend is over
she will be the one
who cries, knowing without knowing
the changes she has wrought.

     5.
And so your story is first told to me
words to be repeated years
to catch the pure light of what happened.

You point to the Cumberland Gap,
the pass that opened the West.
This is where I am from, we lived
right in it

small Appalachian towns,
Southern Baptists and neighbors in trances,
revivals, the handling of
snakes

and the water
that covered everything
my mother when I was ten
drowned herself in this lake
created by the Tennessee Valley Authority

I felt no grief or panic,
didn't cry when my brothers found the note.
Only as the day moved slowly toward night
did I begin to know
she's not coming home.

In your eyes I begin to read
the note she left on the kitchen sink
addressed to the silence of husbands and sons.
Instead of my story
I tell you of my oldest friend in Moab.
She was divorcing her husband
but with the uranium boom for the hydrogen bomb
there was no place to move.
The locals rented out chicken coops.
Couples divorcing
had to live together.

And so she went down to the Colorado,
took all the pills given her for sleep
and lay down on the shore of the river she had always feared
and watched its heavy flow
come from the Rockies.

Her great grandfather founded Moab.
He had come, the Bishop, with all his wives
and instructions from Brigham Young
with enough rope to lower the wagons
over the five hundred foot red walls into the valley.

Her grandfather, the Bishop's son, was the town's moonshiner.
Her father, his son, was sixteen when she was born,
an alcoholic who raped her when drunk.

The storyline was clear, she thought.
After the Indians were killed
God went out of this walled-off redhot world
leaving it radioactive. Sinner
became the spiritual alternative.
She herself was choosing sin, having left
her babies back in the trailer.

Let her husband care for them now.
A good man they all said
who was bored with the passion of her soul
and the tight frigidity of her body.
Her body, he sneered, didn't please him anyway.
And he didn't want to hear again
the story of her father.

Men were coming out of her hair now
settling the country but drowning in the river
being dammed south of Deadhorse Canyon.
It meant jobs but she could hear what the river was thinking
and the mountains sucked hollow for bombs.
And everyone was coming here to live.

In the old days wild horses were trapped
out on the narrow ridge. Crazed
for the water winding five hundred feet below
they would leap.

Men were coming out of her hair now
lowering wagons and wives over uranium walls,
then drowning in the river.
Men and women
just as she had learned as a child
the backbone of the country
and it was breaking.

The water covered old asphalt roads, you tell me.
As a boy I followed roads right into the water,
picket fences, old property lines.
The water drowned everything.
They dragged the lake for days for her body.

6.

I sit in the large, front glass window of your van.
You drive.
The rain digs like nails into the dirt road.
The radio plays *Shame to live in a land*
where justice is a game.

87

The redwood snags standing now in meadows
are still larger than most trees.
The road comes into me. Overruns me.
Before I know if we'll make love
you come into me, your story,
the story of this place,
my own, I haven't told.

Years we've driven
this narrow ridge, Albion,
that reminds us of home

the countless trips back and forth across the country
the road we've grown so old on

animal paths, old Indian foot trails
become superhighways, interstates, buffalo

tearing their way across it, covered wagons
covering it, the flesh
our feet have walked upon, the fear
we still have alone at night
of the land

I tell you the stage used to go through here.
Here's the old road.
Two brothers in their eighties live on that ridge.
They came here in 1915 as dropped-out anarchists from World War I.
They vowed never to marry
so as not to bring soldiers into the world.
They say, oh, yes, it is beautiful
but you should have seen it then.

I tell you of my sisters on this ridge,
daughters of Albion who have vowed
never to take this ride with you again.
We come upon loggers preparing their equipment
to cut the *Last One Hundred*
Virgin Redwoods.

I tell you the Indians here
wore abalone to ward off sadness.
I tell you the tap water here is red
from the roots of ancient forests
many believe are still alive.
I tell you of the one hundredth and fiftieth wave,
of tourists who turn their backs to the sea
and then are swept away

I tell you of blowholes and seawater caves
beneath these ridges
twenty miles to Comptche
of swimmers and ships
sucked into them

I don't tell you of my years with him,
of my daughter and my son.
I tell you instead of the woman's heart
entombed in glass on a gravestone
north of town.
I tell you marriages do not last here.

The road is coming into me.
I tell you my consciousness is political.
My heart is a poet's.
I tell you my story
is the grief, the gap, the hopeless work
between the two.

I tell you the Pomos
wore abalone to ward off sadness
and though the moon has passed from me
everytime I look at you I begin to bleed
as from a fresh wound, an ache
for something I gave up long ago.

And you answer
Write a poem for me
a valentine.
for the river, for the Redwoods.
The heart can be used, tell me why
you live on this ridge.

           7.
Loretta says it's the ancient Jewish way.
We have moved here because
we were pushed out of the city.
When we no longer have control here
we will move on again.

But I think we have come home.
We have touched death
and now carry it here like a new infant.

Like the Zunis in their hour
we are drawing lines of sacred cornmeal
all around us. We are learning to sing
though our tongues were cut out long ago.

We are deformed, dislocated, unable to marry,
but we have remained alive and we have come back to this land.
We have brought our hearts to the very end of the world,
to live on this edge as prophets of form, as artists and farmers,
knowing love is not to transcend the horrors we have known,
or the earth we have never loved

but to know and contain them
within our bodies
as when you come into me
it is the body of America you enter,
her dark unwritten stories.

8. My Story

The light foot hears you and the brightness begins
god-step at the margins of thought
        quick-adulterous tread at the heart
Who is it that goes there?

My body explodes from water to the light,
from the panic of my brother
who holds my head down that he might breathe.
My father stands on the shore
his arms folded across his chest.
My eyes meets his eyes.
He stares at me coldly, deadly.
I go under again.
He doesn't see I'm drowning.
He will be sad. I want to protect him
from this tragedy he is creating.

My body explodes from the deep going
between here and the new country,
my *soul wailing up from blind innocence*
into the deprivations of desiring sight.

He keeps fleeing me without a word.
I keep walking around the world in search of him

Where is the man
man enough
to love?

The story is the oldest story
the Story of the Garden:
She wanted to know.
He wanted not to know.

The Bride in the Song of Songs:
I opened to my beloved, but my beloved
withdrew himself
and was gone.
I sought him, but I could not find him.
I called him but he gave no answer.

Isis wandered the world
picking up the pieces of her lover.
What she could not find
were his balls.
She had to become an artist
and sculpt them.

Psyche turned the light on Eros
who gave her everything, but light.
He could only fuck her
in the dark.

But Psyche knows the light of knowledge
is the love she brings.
Psyche knows she loves him
only when she sees him.

9.   For My Husband Preparing to Flee   (After H.D.)

        a.
What can love of land give to me
that you have not?

What is the ocean to me
if you are lost?
What are the ridges
if you walk them not?

What is the North American Plate?
the Mendocino Fault?
the Pacific High?

What is this place to me
if you are lost?
What can strife break in me
that you have not?
What is Mendocino,
Comptche, Albion, Noyo,
the Navarro
pouring west?

        b.
I walk north to Casper
to the bluff above the beach
to see again the woman's heart
entombed in glass.
She wanted to go home to Scotland.
He wanted her heart to stay.

But beneath Cypress I find
toppled stone, the heart
broken.

I drift as fog along the south bluff of Main Street,
a wet heavy tongue
in the vanished flesh of old Chinatown.
I drift between broken hovels and shapes,
the smells of cooking food,
the shouts and stories
of the thousands who came for gold,
of the thousands who were born here
but shipped their bodies back
to lie forever in China.

What is love of land
you've never seen?
What is my heart
if you don't want it?
Where are the countries
in our flesh?
What is the greatest taboo?
To bring your eyes
to your lover's genitals,
to bring your eyes
to your lover's eyes?

c. Ramon

He stands at the door, calls my name.
His face is not hidden from me.
His body opens, union
not just in a dark, secret place
but full-bodied, the past
still here, those
who do not leave.

But who is he to me if you are lost?
What are the redwoods
if your eyes draw back?

What is the coastline
if you take fright?
Terrible, torturous, isolate,
a barren rock.

What are the whales to me
if you hesitate?
What is Earth if you draw back
from the terror
and cold splendor of Love?

10. Ramona

Break open my heart
live in these terrible images with me

Break open my heart
drag the lake for my body

I float in great blood
and red roses
the unsettled wilderness, the light
that is love
passion throws

Break open your heart, stop
Eros from fleeing,
his head and cock in his hands,
through the broken withered hearts of the old country

The Revolution is
our lovelives, break open your heart

let her out of you
let him out of me
let the tree in

Turn around and go back
across this wintery land

Be the opening of the Cumberland
all the widest, open already occurring world
for me to pass into

this land, this broken-hearted
land we have never loved
we have sacrificed everything for
but have never loved

Break open your heart, let me
make our fire there

        11.

In the meadow when I kneel to you
and for the first time take you in my mouth
I feel the fish beating for the cold pulling
of a distant sea

I know you cannot trust me
the kind of passion that threw your mother into the lake

just as I cannot trust you, the violence
and silence I have known of fathers and husbands
the kind of passion that kills Redwoods

but when I lie on top of you
beneath the map of this country
and the rain falls over us
I know us as the Ark
freed to the stories
that call through dark manure
and red carnivorous soils

I think of my grandfather's life
in the drifts of the mines
and my grandmother for whom I am named
Lura drifting through babies and the family farm
that was drowned by the TVA

and my passion is to suck us back

                    before America was born
                    before the land was cleared
                    before our lives were broken

to wilderness
where marriage is possible

and when you come into me
it is the circle of new shoots
from the burnt heart of redwood

and when you come into me
it is a bird fluttering light
down into the drifts of the mines
where my grandfather worked all his life

and when you come into me
it is a fish slivering up through
shafts of light in the dark water's depth
and finding her, brings her back
to her lost child

Love Song For A Man Whose Mother Killed Herself

Your open mouth like the ocean
where you allow me, swimming.
Beneath all things, the Bible says
are the waters
but men don't usually open this way.
They are always ships headed for some horizon, the rescuers

dragging the lake for days for her body, you said.

You have opened yourself so wide
you are the water your mother drowned in.
She lies at the bottom of you,
the dark deep water that covers you.

I see her face sleeping with open eyes
looking towards the sun.
I am wanting

the secret of this watery garden
the secret the leaves hide
and the wind
call it the world
the secret she would not live without.

It is deep going between here and the new country.
In the night we are seen waving back to the shore.
Voices call for us. I emerge
over your body to see the earth in light.

You have opened to me.
You are the first man who has ever opened to me.
Somehow you have made yourself

the man she would not live without.

White Deer In A Field

I watch you from this last car
grow smaller and smaller in the track,
the knotted male perspective
I will always be leaving.

The train circles the Noyo's drifting mouth,
rushes the crimson algae laid here by a wave,
now climbs the coastal slope.
We burst into flowers
that topple headstones,
suck deep into narrow tunnels, "built,"
a voice echoes in the clackety dark,
"by Chinese Coolies."
Now the voice is a man, sunfleshed
in the shadow-checkered aisle.
"This track laid," he says
"to get the trees."

We fall through them, picking up speed,
tree after tree in the slanting sun
pulling me back
to the simple unfolding
of the story, *Why*

when you found me bathing in the pool
did you look at me and not see
the world and your land, sacred
genital to holy mouth, why
your need to haul my body
into property, your land
into pornography, why
your fantasy to love things
to death?

"These woods used to be filled with cabins.
One day someone came out and set them on fire.
People were living here for free."

I look down into a cabin
perhaps only miraculously here.
A woman in a red flannel shirt
holds up a picture
for a man seated on the other side of the room.

I reach through the glass, like water
to hear his voice
given to her beyond the image, within
the fleeing redwoods. Suddenly

a herd of white deer on the right,
their erotic eyes from the cut hills
nearly unbearable.

You Leave

When you leave
I listen to the car
moan all the way down the ridge to the sea.
It is still morning and the sound
of the rain grows louder, crickets
and the tops of trees
begin to scream.

The raindrops hitting the porch
are small explosions of light,
your face
I've never been able to see
running off to mud.

On the news
they tell of the finding
of an adult female body
less than a mile from here
dead about six months.
This rain has uncovered her.

They know it is a woman because
of the jewelry on her bones.
Was it you who killed her?
Is that why you are leaving?

You have left me.
You have taken
even the jewelry from my bones.

Forests

Mornings before I wake
I am making love to you again.
Through my life I am
rising over you and down
to the furry night between our thighs.

When I open my eyes
and try to rise
out of your hands
I fall into furniture
you made for me.
I open our New England curtains

and see the hole
you cut for me through manzanita
rather than cut it down
that I might have a far view
into the western meadow

I move through the room.
I move through years of your body
you have left here in the children.
There are marks of you on my body.
There are few roads across the country
I could take we did not travel together.

The Redwood Empire is now, at best,
second growth,
and I am a giant snag
after you have clearcut the virgin forest

my famous awesome beauty gone
my enormous roots still snarled
everywhere beneath the ground.

Night Mare On Albion Ridge

Nights a large red mare comes through the front.
She makes her way down the twisted path in the woods,
somehow trots the narow strip between the garden fence
and the redwood stumps that are the steps to my front door.
And there she lingers larger than the cabin and redwood snags,
her mare's nose wetting the night, sending her scent to lay
like a dead boy across my body asleep inside.
Even here in Albion she is too large, too free
to roam the ridge like this, through Pygmy and flimsy
third-growth, her tidal weight thrown like the sea
with all its people who have drowned
up on the land and turning into posses,
while you and I are running ahead, dodging bullets,
into the clouds that rise from the river
to cover the moon. Sometimes a foal and a pony
trail her, having followed through the gate
she mysteriously unlocks
and then she is some nightthing with too many hooves,
a crazed herd stampeding the walls
I have tried to build around me
in these dark woods
where my violent soul takes root
from the dreams of you
suddenly here, like fog, covering
everything, the sun.

A neighbor says she used to pasture in the meadow
eating apples in the fall and she returns in search
of the stallion who was here with her. Sometimes
in the day I look up from the fire
to a caped rider atop her
looking surprised himself to be here. I think she returns
to haunt me for some past deed of the people
who lived here before me, an animal so largely dumb
she is like the dead one at her own funeral
who stands beside each grieving relative
telling them she's right   here
but they can't hear her, they will never
hear her again.

The stallion was gelded.
The neighbor says she was sorry
when she saw the two of us,
such a nicelooking couple, moving into this place
no marriage ever survived, now this witch's hut,
this hovel where I stay warm with sticks,
the wreckage strewn by the path of this strange horse
galloping nights as the sea in my veins in fixed flight
of the rumors of murder and suicide
at the deserted nursery she pastures in now
where the azaleas are unwanted business
and bloom too large in the nightwoods.

107° When We Ride Into Town The Week Before Her Birthday

1.

I watch you fall asleep, then lay myself down
around and into you, as against the cool shade
of the coastal range. I whisper in your ear, *darling*...

Outside teenage boys drag Main Street,
drag hunger across town.
I hear all the worlds of the universe,
the dangerous hot wheels, fling into their bodies.

I fall asleep. When the sun goes down
we'll walk Main Street, see the town.
But we sleep all night. In the dream
I wear a red party dress, triumphantly pull
a train down a long track.

At breakfast I watch a family whose bodies
are dark, foreign, the images of dream.
The father sips his coffee next to the son,
looks at me as if into a cool shadowy cave
in which he would like to lie down.

On the table next to our food
Christians storm Palestinian camps.
Three workers sit beneath a buck's head
and a Vacation Bible School poster,
sit like an ancient assemblage of mountains
folded down the dingy room, one behind the other.

You are telling me of the Ancestral Rockies,
how the horse is native to this country
but left a million years ago,
and bison, native to the Orient, migrated here.

They adapted quickly, eating around the wet margins of glaciers.
I look out to Main Street, this long celebration.
How did we ever come here?
An angry old woman comes down the street, waving her arms.
She stops at our window, smiles at herself.

In ancient America the bodies of dead infants
were buried as boundary lines of the great nations.
When I was a child I dug in my backyard for China.
Our lives I've learned since then are bitter convulsions
away from Earth. An arch freezes
across the top of the world
causing the sea level to drop.
A voice whispers *move on, move on.*
We travel to the holy places, *San Francisco,*
Wyoming, Cumberland Gap,
drivers dragging hunger,
foreigners in search of the track that is known to go there,
for the voice we know we hear,
darling....

2. Prayer For The Beginning of A Journey

O most passionately and deeply
make this earth visible
within me

Take me
over and over
incessantly
to those who have proceeded me
to those who come after

Plunge me into deepest earth
and let me bring back
to that wider, widest circuit
what is seen and heard

Fourth of July

We are in a dream
taking the bus
traveling to find her
though no one seems to know
who she is.

We arrive at the beach.
For as far as anyone can see
white combers are rolling in.
Someone points to the sea.
A lion is arching out of the water
into the great welcoming arms of the sky.
And then everything changes

and many beasts are rising
from the roaring surf, immense silver bears subdividing
turning upright on hindlegs
filling the sky with the living pounding sea, until, *tombs,*
bearers of light, streams down spacious skies, they are
the light, the frontier risen

in monumental solidity, in phosphorescent solemnity, more
powerful, more beautiful, more magnificent, more loving
than anything we have known

From the Revolution of time and water, across nothing
they stare at us.
Giants. Their divine eyes
sitting in immense flesh
open on us
as if to say

Yes, we are here.
We are
as we are. Surely
you are not surprised.

But we, subdividing in the shadows of their great lit forms,
their shocking love, we are circling,
scattering down the beach, hungering
for what could be in darkness,
yearning toward some violence
we can imagine

pull knives from our clothes and turn,
in the grinding, civil light,
on each other

You and I run.
We run away.

occurred July 4-5, 1976

Bicentennial

You came.   A History

and covered my face with your breath
With your breath
        you raised me beyond
        the body of my own breathing

A tree sprouts
from my buried heart
America's images take place in my bones
in the World's valley, low
and open

I am the streets the people walk
the terrible streets we have walked in countless dreams
of towns and cities
whose names and locations we didn't know

In my love
I am the history of this country
what no human heart can bear
Loved in effigy, I lie down
unforgiven
in earth

and wait

        for the Revolution
        your Breath
        pulling dead Indians from the soil

Part III
HEARTLAND

The way geography moves around inside a couple.

Jack Hirschman

It was crossing the country for the first time by car that made
me a Revolutionary.

Jane Fonda

When the children of your children's children
Think themselves alone,
Tell them:
Wherever they may be:
Upon the prairies, in the broad lands,
In their cities of stone,
Upon the highroads that cross the land:
Wherever they may be:
They will not be alone.
When the streets of the strange cities you have built
And are yet to build
Are empty, silent, and deserted,
They will be crowded with ghosts who shall return
To walk the earth we left to you and them,
For we still love this land and even
Death will not take this from us.
When we are gone and you are everywhere,
We will walk still the land we love.
The white man will never be alone.

Seattle

Metamorphosis

When you fall asleep
your head at my belly
I stare at the ceiling.

Time pases and your dark hair passes
to that of another I still love
who must be traveling now
this dry hot state alone
a thousand miles to the south.

My body is cast here in a strange city
like an outlaw seeking a new identity.
But the blood in my veins
is still on the run, drains after him,
the dry arroyos of the state.

Why did I tear myself from him?
In the sleep of those wanted
dead or alive
I dream what is left here is blood
and *this*, my real mouth.

Avenue of the Giants

The cars travel
the mystical highway north
through iridescent, silver-blue columns.
While loggers haul south
Trees of Mystery
still so virgin
only one will fit
on each bed.

The last giant wanders the world,
hunted, looking for its mate.
You hike the Mad River,
catch Sasquatch at her bath.
In the trembling bud of the moment
you stare at each other
across the rapids.
It occurs to you
she is shy.

When she throws herself
into the fur of the mountain
there comes a shattering scream

unlike any sound ever heard

one that lays bare
to every creature in the wood
the human story.

She Is A Flock Of Birds Rising

She remembers a windy rest area years ago
in the desert of the Colorado
With the children sleeping beside them
they did it silently in the wind

Now she is with this new man
They lie down on the highway
In the low hum of the travelers still on the road
and the diesels running all night
while the truckers sleep
they perform a dance in the tall pines
to the global wind
coming in from the sea

She looks at him and she remembers
when she first saw him standing at her door
She knew she once
looked through his eyes

Now he touches her
They both undress her
He takes her from the floor of the highway
and raises her
to her truelove's eyes
to his hands that reach for her

Like birds that rupture blood vessels
when the excitement of song is upon them
now they are a flock of birds rising
to the whistling tops of trees
that sway all night in the global wind
coming in from across the sea

And now they hear
the earth rolling in the wind beneath them
gathering and seizing
And now in their bodies
they hear
her laughing

I'm coming open

My Mother Is A Poem I'll Never Write

He couldn't wait to meet my mother.
He kept saying you'll never know
who your woman is
until you meet her mother.
He said it so often he angered me, he, a safe
orphan, with his mother self-drowned.

But I think he must see me
as she is walking in this light
down from her home to meet us,
an orphan herself, but as awesomely clear
as anything on this Oregon coast.
Even I can feel myself as she comes
carried in that wide house between her hips.

My mother is a poem I'll never be able to write
though everything I write is a poem to my mother

of whom he later said as we were leaving
And your mother, oh, your mother
Deep. Deep water. The waters run deep.

Letter To Ramona

1.

We are twenty-three miles south of Coos Bay on a sheltered beach
which took us two hours to find. He plays his harmonica.
Against the sun that breaks open wider and wider
like an old rose losing its petals, a young man hotrods
the dunes. Two small children hang on to the backseat.
The wife rides, mute and still beside him, a dark
silhouette, her mannequin head, a beady satellite
of the sun.

2.

When I lived in Vermont a woman from this town
was sentenced first to death and then to life
in a Turkish prison for smuggling hashish.
Across the sub-zero hillside of northern Appalachia
came the sunbluffs and islets, the white-ribboned blue Pacific
of Coos Bay. And a prison wall without windows.
I heard the sentence so that everything started
and the beaches of my childhood
came through the courtroom haze
and my body was breaking open
the story I'd never live.

3.

We had coffee in Port Orford across from Battle Rock
my husband and son climbed years ago.
In this history the whites were stranded, the Indians charging
when the tide came in. The sea
saved them. Suddenly, the small body of my son
came to me, not as memory
but the young boy charging like a glorious brave
in our tribe's last victory.
From then, he came to me now, a life sentence.

Between us and Battle Rock, inaccessible at high tide,
a soldier was hitching. The sun had burnt on his face
the belief that no one was going to stop. When he looked
I waved and remembered the teenage waitress
from that time: *I hate this place. A prison,*
her words like angry gulls scrying over the Earth's
most beautiful presentation of itself, charging me,
in her stillbirth, a year later, with Turkey. Prison. Hashish.

4.

Fact. Real dream. They melt on our bodies
like the sun on this beach as it descends.
The sea will save the sun, hold light after darkness.
I sit in the car, mute, sentenced, as he rides me north
a grinning thief with his loot.
All the continent east of here
leans on me in this rare moment of my life.
I don't know what to do. Where else to go.

5.

The sun drowns, causing the old distortions, the sharp-
edged illusions, the Grand Canyon in the sky.
Harmonica. Harmonious lines of Earth, she turns
and returns, catches you in these places
that remember you. The local paper tells of this town's
great hope, the long-distance runner, dead in a car crash
the night he broke the American record. The local paper
is called the World.

Insomnia

1.

When he falls asleep I open the van door.
Night looks in. For a long time I watch
three cars and a pick-up race and spin
across a silver-lit giant searock
whose legs straddle this Coos Bay sealip.
The cave is filled with moon and sloshing sea
as in the ancient rites of women
who opened their legs on midnight beaches
while husbands dilated vaginas open
until, the sea coming, Moon's ray
could enter.

2.

John Donne looked upon his *continual waking*
as rehearsal for the life to come
when we will always want to be awake.

Now I'm rocked against the whine, unwind
of their ceaseless machines, the ocean's ker-*boom*.
These Oregon orphans adrift a lunar beach:
their vulgar squeals, their mag wheels, their Oly's.
The mad play of young men. Hum me, chugalug,
a lullabye.

3.

Moonray, their headlights
fall on us.
He turns, curses me
still awake.

Close the door. Night.
Night like a river that's damned.
Like Isis, cursed. To be delivered
in no month or year.
Washed in the grind of gravel, bent
beneath waves. Close your eyes,
see the boy inside
hitching south.

Kerouac and Monroe on Kalaloch

1.

Long ago they found each other here.
She wanted to be like the wild stallion
she had seen in Nevada. He had lost his mind
in Massachusetts.

They sat all day on the long beach.
They drank beer propped against drowned trees.
Sometimes they spoke. Mostly
they stared at the sea. Low tide. High.
Their famous faces flared on the screen of the sky.
Their faces grew tired, turned red.
Their limbs dried. The sun fell. They became
driftwood. They were dying. She said
tell me of sex.

He recited Rilke's Ninth Elegy.
She heard only the line
and escapes
in ectasy
beyond the violin.
Tell me, she cried, of when
you were a kid.

2.

She slid her hand down the haggard belly, held him.
He was warm. He stirred. He stayed small.
He slept. She watched twelve pelicans
row the horizon. She laid her head
on the blade of his shoulder.

She saw his face above the waves.
It was the saddest face she had ever seen.
She saw the face held knowledge
of her death. She saw the man
might be the man
who murders her.

They walked miles up the beach
looking for a bed.
He quoted poets who had slept here.
He said he knew the island was Tatoosh
from the poems. He said poets
find their lovers here. Later,
they found a road sign. It named the island
Destruction.

3.

In a tavern on the highway an Indian was saying
Hunting elk is a disease. I seen
an elk hunter pump seven bullets
into an elk that wasn't there.
And he didn't even have
his gun.

Tell me about sex, she said
as they drank. Tell me
who you are. He said, I've been
ruthless.

The bartender asked, Where you two from?
You look familiar, like a couple I know
in Wyoming. The Indian went on
You can take any road out of here,
sleep over night, hear them,
the mating calls, cougar, lynx, black bear
this time of year.

They walked back through slashpiles.
It was dark. He said
I learned to be ruthless
from the Church. I took
a vow of poverty.

She searched the sky for the southern stars.
She saw how far she had come.
Shit. She said, I was born
in L.A.

        4.
They made a bed beneath Cedar
on a bluff above the sea.
She would have preferred the beach.
He was afraid of rain.
She was glad to know
of something he felt.

They made a small fire.
They cooked soup in the can.
They covered themselves with a single blanket.

        5.
When first they loved
when her body lifted off the needles
when her body rose and churned like the demonic waves
when her cries, lifted to the night,
screamed back at them like gulls

she knew why
no man
had ever stayed with her.

In her shame she begged for his shirt.

        6.
When second they fucked, she sobbed.
She screamed. It was not
pleasure. He folded his arms around her back,
lifted her from the ground.
The water rolled from her face. He said
What is my name?

7.

When they loved again she remembered
this may be the man who kills me.
She felt his hands
form the body she knew as a girl.
She saw the racoons watching them.
In star's light their needles glistened.
She thought
Cougar. Lynx. Black Bear

and such a light body he laid on her
So thin. His ribs. He was hard to find.
He fled more than she. Are you ever...
she searched Cedar for the word
Emotional. When he was through
he poured his dark face into her pale hair.
She felt his body heave
in the attempt to cry.

8.

She watched the Virgin slip into the water.
She woke him. Tell me about
ruthless.

He told her. She lay quiet. This man
could kill her. She watched
the Scales of Love go down.
She woke him. She whispered
don't be ruthless
with me. You can get
whatever you want
without being
ruthless.

He promised. He slept. Of course, she said
to the Scorpion, I can
take it. He was awake. He said
I know you can.

9.

Once from the night she heard the Indian again.
Wednesday is hump night. That's half-way
over the hump. She saw the racoons
getting ready. Cougar. Black Bear. She said
Ruthless means
a promise
is nothing.

He was awake. He said
I know. I thought of that.

10.
When again they loved, as the Hunter
drowned, as the night rolled over
the hump of the sun, he shook her shoulders
and cried, Do you even
know my name?

11.
In the silver light of morning, at the coldest hour
they loved again. The tide was high. Water
rushed the bluff. Cedar flared above them.
He buried his mouth
in the wild yellow grass
between her legs.
The seasons changed. It was summer
when they met. Now the trees flamed
and fell.

12.
He took his shirt from her.
He leaned over the bluff.
The sky and sea found his body
for her. Tell me, she said,
about sex.

He put on his black leather cap.
The saddest face she had ever seen
smiled. He said, My name is Jack.
Your name is Marilyn.
And that is why we sojourn here
alone on Kalaloch.

13.
They are so far from home.
She says his name. He touches her lips.
She will escape into ectasy beyond the violin.
When he can't cry, he will see his own face
above the waves, he will shoot
fictitious elk, he will be without his
gun. He will be ruthless.

Oregon

As Clark and Sacajawea walked onto the sands
to view a stranded 105 foot whale
the bad news broke upon them.

There were no ships to carry them home.
They would have to return overland.

1.
The Columbia is wide and we ride
her banks and gorges east, through stacks
stories high, through treacherous   falls

Around the bend
snow-covered volcano. Cone.
Iconic. Mythic
Washington

The first sign Lewis and Clark had
of the Pacific Ocean

was an Indian walking on shore
wearing a pea coat

At the Dalles
the Bridge of the Gods collapsed.
The trail ended. As far as you
could go. Now the Cascades.
You had to convert your wagons
to rafts.

Floated then to the Rim
through eons, through rivered-down palisades
through sun
down basalt pillars

Even before white man, flying
saucers were seen on this river

2.
Upon the rock face
another face, painted blue, howls
with torch, feathers

From the falls the Bride
leaps, to save her lover
when the sickness
comes on his face

Across the river, Coyote's
Unattached Penis, hurled
to the princess

On the beach
that winter
they found the coastal tribes

dying
the sailor's disease, the
crooked walk, syphilis

3.

Last night I dreamed I lived on this river.
Returning home
the earth tilted
and the winds were blocked.

I slipped off into a forbidden time
following on old couple
up a dry, inaccessible canyon
to their cabin.

Halfway there I saw
I had no way of ever
returning.

4.

Five stars came down from the sky
and slept here beside the river.

One of the five did not go back.
He remained on the shore
as a white flint rock,
large, round, thick and bright.

The people here became known as the Star People.
They were prosperous, lucky
until the jealous people on the other side
smashed the star into pieces
and threw him into the river.

But this is why the Columbia
sparkles.

5.

Spray drifts across our river highway
Pillars of Hercules, the train
running between Coyote's children

Beacon Rock, his oldest son,
one of the largest monoliths in the world

wanted the girl with the beautiful hair.
Coyote, annoyed, fastened her
to the side of the mountain
turned her hair

into Maidenhair Falls. Now always fleeing,
she never gets away.

6. The Bridge of the Gods: The Fall
1843

I can hear the sound of rapids, the boat rising and falling.
I can see the breakers ahead, broken lines extending across the way.

The pilot squats low in the bow. An old red handkerchief
is tied around his head and his long black hair hangs down his back.

Now breakers on the right and on the left. Foam-crested waves
sweep across our bow. The motion of the boat is so delightful,
an exaggeration of the cradle and grapevine swing combined.

I begin to think this is no ordinary rapid. But the old people
sit quietly in their places, betray no sign of fear.

The two babies fall asleep in their mother's arms, rocked
in the heaving river-bosom, lulled by the medley of sounds.

Then I look across the river and see the smaller boat on the south bank.
Why are they over there? The pilot is with us
and he has warned, this is the dangerous part.

And then a wail of anguish, a shriek, and a scene of confusion
in our boat no language can describe. We see the boat disappear,
the men and boys struggling in the water

and above the roar of the rushing waters Mother and Aunt
by commands and entreaties bring Father and Uncle to know

of the madness to swim to the other side. Let them go.
Let the sons go.

7. Thirty Thousand Remain Along The Oregon Trail

One grave for every
one hundred yards

from the Missouri to the Willamette
only a few have been found

the trail to Oregon through
garbage heaps, the trail
of the last train

wells and latrines, too close, seepage
and stink, guns
discharged
in the jolting wagons,
children bounced out
trampled
by stampeding cattle
the next wagon

At the end of the day's ride

bury them
leave no trace

Start out again in the morning.
Each wagon roll over them.
Don't let the savages know.
Never come this way again.

8. Pioneer

O, wild-girl wilderness, thrown seed
though they tried
to make you a vessel, a bed
instead of a road

One day in the middle
you finish the quilt

but keep on stitching

pointless, blinding compaction
of stitches, the madness
of your crossing.

Days
advancing to that bluff.
Then. Coming around it, like coming
through a door:
Sun

on the floor, a blue movement.
Shadow of bird's flight
the only trail

9. Migration

You can hear on the wind
the voice of a boy calling

His body with all colors of light
is surounded by light

a new world coming
in a whirlwind
out of the west, warm Chinook

lifting the bed
of the Columbia

Oregon
a whirl up from the guts and
flexing heart

Oregon, you are not easy
to enter

One must know
the secret
by heart

      10.   The Labor of Pioneers
        a.
My water breaks
No other sign
Just the silent letting down
of great rivers

in the light of Venus
and the new moon swallowed
by Blue Mountains, my body's
time. Of course

you are coming. Here. Now. Night.
Without country.

        b.
You can hear
the earth cryng.
The stars are small doors
you strain to get through
to comfort her.

She sobs about that
landmark. Stars smashed
into pieces. Thrust up
like knees, the world's
largest monolith.

Mouth
full of rocks.

        c.
Your outline in the sun
that rises. Skin against the country
I carry,   heat

waves rise and decay, rhythm
of your migration, passenger
out of the shapeless maw

Waxing and waning of the World.
Geological. Epochs. Rock. Soul. The whole
motion before my eyes, creation
to conclusion. Ruins.

d.

O, ill-winds handed me in a bag,
unformed beginning
To inhale is to exhale
boulders, buried

O, birdness, most majestic, Trickster,
Creator, Destroyer, the whirl-up

from the geocentric guts
and flexing heart

o, missionary, little fish
out of water.

e.

Of course you come here
now. Osiris-torn, many eyes
through bones so still

you are the slow journey
west

You see the sun set. The sun sees
your genitals. Aflame.
I gather up

your small white parts, your missing
chord. Boy.

f.   American Ruin

Carry the dead boy
wrapped beneath
milk
coming in

Don't let anyone know
until we get to a station

His eyes sink
like small nail heads
in soft wood

The day shrinks.
As we advance, look back
to the stairs of our leaving.
Mark the path.

I promise
I'll find you again.

Tenant. Son. Crow.
Little boy of this
country. Gull

flying into the black clouds.

Idaho

1.

The deepest erosion scar of the continent
where Chief Joseph and the Nez Perce
crossed the Snake

The River of No Return
where Marilyn sang
I cried a river for you

Ea-da-how: *The Sun Comes Down The Mountains*
that block cold blasts from Canada

He says *Think of a seagull's flight to Idaho.*
Instinctual feelings, the Pacific
used to lap right up to the Rockies.

2. Boise

She hurries through downtown streets to meet her lover,
the wind whipping her skirt
like a flag around her.   Ghosts
in the golden dome capitol, in the woodwork
of small houses: *You must remember*
our dismembered parts.

The Chamber of Commerce boasts
Idaho is what America used to be.
Sherwood Anderson in a bookstore:
I've got a grey and ragged brother
in my breast. That's a fact.

3.

A woman stares at herself
in the shiny armor of a knight
astride a white horse,
a postcard entitled *Reflection.*
I write to Loretta

She looks into his armor
and sees herself.
This is the way the people look here
beneath this sky
which everywhere reflects back
the small western knot
of the self.

Tourists Out of Season

Up in old Idaho City, as the sun falls,
the houses sit, propped in summer, small.

A baby cries in the hundred year old dredge
piled up along every road and creek bed.
The museum expresses its condolences.
The librarian says no one ever reads here.

But the birds sing. He captures in his box
this goldmining town, self-conscious, turning
like all the genuine places
to tourist attraction, the people so hungry
for authenticity.

The air begins to pain. The couple talk:
what it must have been like. They walk the town,
dream inside history marks. A curtain
with a white arm folds back as they come.

They have broasted Idaho potatoes in a dark saloon
decorated for the ski crowd. The doorsign warns
of danger to your heart. Out on the street
she has to return, through men who turn, slack-jawed,
to call her sister
backhome. They take her picture.

In the park they sit on old mining equipment
wondering what to do.
Three boys on bikes race toward Idaho's oldest jail.
A teenage boy comes out of the house too small,
and across the infant green
practices his guitar, dreams
of getting out. Firecrackers from the jail
rip the dusk. The sound
of laughter from boys.

Idaho Is What America Used To Be

1.

Insomnia. Prairie schooners. Taut
sails. How could anyone sleep?
We've come to the middle of the country.
The ruts of the Oregon Trail
still lead into the desert
miles.

2.

We've placed our bags
as close to water as possible.
Stars burn like tears
through White Pine,
the state tree. Small fires
burn my face. You lay
between us. I hear you
like the breathing of horses
heard a mile away in deep winter.

3.

Flight of wagon trains crossing strange borders.
Now in wilderness semen is gold.
The Bridegroom's spent. He flees.
She's married dust. Greed.

4.

The creek burns all night
through hundred year old dredge.
He speaks in his sleep
through the dredge of men
who replaced gold with the real thing.
The miles spread out in me, dry dust
of a dozen states grinding
to black asphalt sleep. I've come,
the martyr of sage and rock,
with the wrong man. Night waits
for the raid. In the north, rain.
Cry me, she sang, a river
of no return.

Insomnia: Somewhere The Four Corners of the Sioux

When I was a girl
the books I read were by men
written while their women and children slept
and I vowed I would write books
as the woman awake
while my man and children slept

because that's the way it's always been

Now I lie on the floor beside him
in a small stucco house
on the outskirts of Boise.
He is asleep. Everyone is asleep.
The hard, unyielding floor and the room spins,
meanness, betrayal, spite, someone else's wound.
I could never have borne it.

You cry under the redwoods
south of here, your shoulders collapsed.
Again, you tell me why
you are leaving
as soon as you fix my car.

Miles to the north a blazing man
whose rainbow colored flesh fills the yellow clouds
pulls me from our daughter's bed
through the window
in the direction of the storm.

But he slips. I slip.
The jolt wakes me,
deadwhite, betrayed,
still on the floor.

I travel east with our son
in search of you.
You rise out of reach,
too large, turning red,
like the white buffalo
who left through a hole in the sky
when they saw us coming.

I wake and do not know who sleeps,
his back to me,
or in what black night I'm birthing
the child. I hold my elongated hands
beneath the foreign bulge
as I emerge from the Pacific.
Red, yellow, white, black, together
is brown, the color
of the fifth race.

Sometime just before light,
thunder and rain.
A horse whinnies in the corral.
The room spins
a world where
what was sleeping
is now awake.

Leaving Boise: Retreat

What lays waste my heart
lays waste, lays waste my art

1.
Across a faraway plain, devoid of heart, the couple moves out
against a voice that chants *don't go on, don't go on*

Across the Camas Prairie they proceed
Owyhee, Sawtooth, Nez Perce,
Bannock, Blackfoot, Blood

At Mountain Home they turn north and east
through Goodale's Cutoff: *to avoid Indian hostility*

In the shadow of streaming clouds
atop the flickering global frontier
they read how Buffalo Horn's band
went to war, fought clear to central Oregon
before returning, defeated
to Idaho

Now the stars turn to cruelty,
Saturn rings their suffering:
What she did

North, around Magic Reservoir, Shoshone
ice caves, the much-imagined land
of an old commune from the Twenties,
the Sixties retreat of her Southern California friend
the place she kept meaning
to drop out to

the I Am Church, people who believe

I AM   I AM

and in star people

Three generations now
have seen and talked to them, gone abroad
unidentified flying objects.
Women who don't know
who the fathers are

her California friend
trying to touch winter

this wide-open silver Camas Prairie
guaranteed by treaty

        2.   The Poet's Retreat
She follows the path of the Nez Perce
across Washington, Idaho, Montana
because she has retreated herself
from the war and the country
ten years to heal the heart
on the mountains and beaches
of Ramona, Topanga, Ojai,
Vermont, Albion, Mendocino.

She comes to the first place of massacre.
The night is still and clear.
She lies on the ground to sleep.
A wind comes up.
She ignores it.
The wind grows fiercer.
The wind seems to blow
at her.

Then she sees as in a dream
the old woman from the mountains of Ojai
who retreated years ago
after her left breast had been removed
and then was told
her right one would also be taken.

She bolted from her suburban home
for the mountains to die
as she had never lived.

But through the many years
she was seen at least once every season
stepping to the shore above bathers
in the winter hot springs
or from the pungent summer sage
on a trail made by deer.
In the valley below she became known as
Califia the Amazon
the mythic California woman
who removes her breast
to more precisely
aim the bow.

Now she steps forward
to the poet sleeping on the ground.
The mountains light up.
Her chest is one breast,
brown and like a warrior's,
slung to the waist,
and a green stem
twisting up the rocky spine of the scar
to a small tattooed bud, a wild rose
where the nipple once came.

My name is One.

Behind her the male poets
play the bonegame.
As the dice is thrown
they chant

you are white
you are a woman
you are not to sleep
in these places

We forbid you
to write of them

And the one who died in Viet Nam
bends to her, touching the place
between her thighs.
You remember me. I'm Ramon,
the one you loved first.

And the male poets gamble and jeer.
We were born here.
We killed ourselves here.
We killed everything
for you. We forbid you
to write of this.

3.   I AM   I AM
Joseph said *I don't want to die in a strange land.*

Looking Glass, brave old
Too-hool-hool-zote,
Ollikut, the genial giant

Five Wounds, White Bird, Red Echo and
Rainbow

led them out
the 150 mile Lolo Trail
that led toward the plains

They jammed their ponies through a cruel and arduous route
rising to altitudes of 10,000 feet
leaving a path marked by blood,
abandoned animals with broken legs
or stretched dead
by the wayside

Later the soldiers noted
scarred trees along the route
where the fugitives had been so hungry
they had eaten inner bark

Emerging from Lolo Canyon they entered
the cliff-sided narrows of Bitterroot Valley
and found their way blocked by a sturdy timber barricade,
35 soldiers, 200 volunteers, and a party
of Flatheads

but about 10 o'clock we heard singing
apparently above our heads. Upon looking up
we discovered the Nez Perce passing along the side of the cliff
where we thought a goat could not pass
much less an entire tribe of Indians with all their impedimenta.
The entire band dropped into the valley beyond us
and then proceeded up the Bitterroot.

4.   Who Are The Fathers?
In the history museum at Hailey she finds
no mention of Ezra Pound
though his burial in Venice is temporary.
His last poem, his will, specifies
his body to be returned
to Hailey, Idaho,
his portrait bust by Gaudier-Brzeska
to be his tombstone.

The hills rise up
perfectly peaked and barren
to enclose the future fragments
shored against our ruin

He was born here
near the cold deadend
when the earth turns in its deepest stardense frame,
seared in the instant
by too much space and bald land.
The quest: to find his place inside
with the others
around the court's fire.

Mrs. Pound was a beautiful woman, well-bred, somewhat
affected in manner. One was inclined to be embarrassed and baffled
by her witticisms, her epigrams, as one so often was by Ezra's.
Mr. Pound was hearty, informal, very kind,
a government assayer at the Philadelphia Mint.
He invited a group of us to visit the inner sanctum.
He showed us minute weights and measures, explained
the analysis of gold---
> *"There,"   and he unlocked a heavy door...*
there were stacks of gold bars---
> *"Here,"*
and coins were piled in neat rows,
> *"will you help yourself," chuckling*
heartily.

Has anyone ever noted, reported, or even known this?
It seems to me that Homer Pound's government job in Philadelphia
played an extravagant part in Ezra's later compulsions.
Usury? Usura.... I don't mean that Ezra wanted the gold for himself.
He wanted to change the world with it.

She moves through deep corridors
to Ketchum, to Hemingway,
through his impersonalism, his sexism,
his anti-semitism, his elitism, his fascism

his worship of rulers, Church saints and educated
men, his vanity, his insanity, his endless namedropping, his
usury

She moves through her comrades too-forgiving acclaim
the greatest Twentieth Century poet
because she knows
the love of beauty above the human
is fascism

She moves through deep corridors,
the apparition of his faces in the hills:
scorpion in the dry, black sage.

Go to Idaho, Ernest.
Ea-da-how: The Sun
Comes Down The Mountains

If the reds kick you out of Cuba
go fish, fight and fuck
and kill yourself in Ea-da-how.
The Twentieth Century after all is the primitive.
Incoherence, mindlessness, the caves, the ruled.
Not my rules and rulers.
Not this dead meat, this continent's cultured carcass
rotting in me. You the one,
I the few, said John Adams
to his volatile friend, Mr. Jefferson.
(to break the pentameter, that was the first heave.)
Hang it all, Ernest, I've been the American Innocent Abroad!
The Irish Catholic had it right
when he killed us in Daedelus, birthed from our corpse
his jew-boy, Leopold.

She moves through what she loves well,
this wild American place of his birth,
the other's death
and remembers the future, the scorpion as phoenix,
when they both are here.

     5.   Papa
They move through deep corridors to Ketchum.
He takes her picture
in front of the Old Man's monument.
She learns of his last day.

As I was undressing in the big room upstairs
I sang out the old Italian lovesong

"Tutti mi chiamano bionda.
Ma bionda io non sono."

And Ernest in his room joined me,

"Porto capelli neri."

He knew he was always welcome in my bed.
Goodnight, my lamb, I called.
Sleep well.
Goodnight, my kitten, he answered.

The sounds of a couple of drawers
banging shut
woke me the next morning.
Dazed
I went downstairs
saw the crumpled heap

bathrobe and blood
the shotgun lyng
in the disintegrated flesh

6. Reflection

She drives them out, against the people
who strain at the borders
seeking forgiveness.

In the mirror, the deadblue eye
that reflects all that can't be absorbed,
she sees, through the blond frame of her hair,
craters of the Moon, Lost River Sink,
miles of black lava flow
in the fissure zones

a prairie schooner tilting in the wind,
a legendary ship sailing around the Great Rift,
Icarus falling to the City of Rocks,
populated by a people
whose only hope
is to sash their withered hearts
to Atomic City.

No wonder they believe in star people here,
those who fall into our history
but see us so clearly
they are seen through. Everywhere
you can feel the longing
to break through
all that can't be absorbed.

The Self, *my lamb, my kitten*
who begins to disquise itself
porto capelli neri,
as it approaches
self-realization.

Utah

I want to go there
to my oldest friend
drop myself south down the Snake River Plain
lower myself down like her great grandfather the Bishop
lowered wagons and wives down red Moab bluffs

I want to drop myself down the Wasatch Range
let her take me into her old farmhouse, her thirteen children
the way last night the night and the pines took me
sleeping along the side of the road to the Tetons

I want to hug the road all the way
the way she, a Jack Mormon convert
took her young Cherokee husband dead on a mountain road
beneath the great Timpanogos

and lay down on the blood stain like a bed of his body bent
around the curve in the mountains
the too-tilted floor that flung him out of his life, leaving her
wife to the asphalt path over the mountains
to the oilfields and boomtowns
that we may keep traveling the highways

I want to go there
yet my car keeps moving north and east away
from the crowds on Provo streets where we walked the next day
all the way to Salt Lake City, opening her arms, breathless,
to the people walking towards us,
a strange exhilaration, I just want
to take everyone, the world
into my arms,

and he in Heaven now
learns to be God
waits for her to be through with this earth, these latter days
prepares a galaxy for her the Queen to lie down in
where the children then to come from her body
will be the planets of a new universe
they will be Gods of

I want to go there
yet my car keeps moving north and east away from her
on this old highway not yet widened I traveled as a girl
to the heart of America.
I look down the south side of the country
west over the mountains from the Colorado River that shaped him
to where he lies now above the Great Salt Lake
once thought to be the Pacific Ocean
The Body of her young Lamanite
the Rockies risen in him now, a lost copper mine
becoming salt now, becoming seagulls

The Heart of America: Yellowstone

1.

There were no maps or charts beyond the Mandan villages of the Missouri.
What knowledge there was of the far Rockies was more myth than fact---
legends of live mammoths wandering through deep canyons, of solid salt
mountains hundreds of miles long, of giants so fierce they killed all
intruders upon their domains.

2.   California Seagulls Fly Here To Mate

Fountain Paint Pots
hotsprings and geysers

Through the sulfurous steam
the couple argues
you brought every ghost with you

We hurry from landscape to spectacle.
I lean into the boiling pools, am steamed
in his memory

the dark precise dancer, the terrible
lost boy, his refraction of grace,
the violent bending of his great form over me,
winged and beating

3.   She Wonders Why They Don't Film Gothic Romances Here

Heartstained   Yellow
stone. Fissures and fractures

though I run with this man
the country and back
I cannot escape the man I love

We direct our words around
steam vents and fumaroles.
Gases rush from fireholes.
Rainbow-bursting bubbles lob mud on the rail,
his hand.
Asshole! He brought me home
for you to fuck!

Molten rock. A season in Hell.
Near here
is the way to go down.
I didn't know
this anger was in me:

Old Faithful! Buffoon! Scapegoat! nervy
Eros! You
are the landscape
between us.

4. Her Husband
He comes walking here out of an old song.
His hair flies seagulls, silhouetted
semaphore against the sun.
Then demilune and claustral
he breaks off,
a particle
passing through the hissing chambers of my mind.

He touches a tree, *Coyote...*
I migrate toward him. *Trickster!*
Clouds
He vanishes into the valleys

What is this place to me if he is lost?

I hear his voice in the voices around me.
Mirror! I can find no shield he does not shatter,
no place to hide from his look.

5. The World's Tallest Geyser
Far across the sun it begins to rain.
The souls coming back splash on us
as warm, heavy drops. Shudder
of Creation, caberet mirror, honeycombed

by senuous roots of spring
and the anger of grizzly
smelling menstrual blood

But he came to me on the run.
Harlequin, dealer, pornographer, ex-con.
Our marriage: his lucky hideout.

6. *The Heart of America: How Do We Spend The Centuries?*
    a. He Explains
The continents began sliding around.
North America, moving northwestward,
ran into a mountain range on the floor of the Pacific Ocean,
the East Pacific Rise.

Some of America ran right up the side of the mountain
and down the other, overriding the East Pacific Rise.

Yellowstone: a hotspot on the ocean-peak
            over which North America slipped.

Heartstained: the heat created from the friction,
            a melt in the crust.

America is always coming from the East,
overriding everything in her path,
this trail of heat, this Snake
River basalt, this hot trail
melting the way as we slide
faster to the west
down the backside of the great range
now beneath the Rocky Mountains.

    b.   She Understands
Ancient layered American heart,
your wounded land: Purple

heartsickening, heartwounded land within me, your
Continental fold

Yellowstone, destined to head further east
eventually to get out into
Kansas and Nebraska

    7.   Vietnamese Tourists At Heart Lake
(On the Mirror Plateau in Yellowstone National Park, the retreating Nez
Perce, led by Chief Joseph, encountered a group of tourists on vaction
from the east.)

I have jewelry   I have gold
I hardly knew a war was going on

cell by cell, I remake myself

a nervous ache, an act of
treason

    8.   Love The One You're With
Volcanoes showered the region with ash and rock.
Lavas flowed across the land to form the bulk of the plateaus.
Ice buried the land, glaciers grinded over the plateau
into the Valley of the Firehole.

Ice pushed over the hot springs only to melt so rapidly
great heaps of gravel formed.

How do we spend the centuries?   Rilke asks
Nature speaks not of love.

Nature bears it in her heart
and no one knows
the heart of Nature

and I am the boy who fell in this boiling pool
the summer I came here with my husband
and you are your mother
self-drowned in the cold Cumberland

9. Old Faithful

Still, I come open to the figure of you,
a young man standing near the source of the pool

Hot waters cascade
through a series of delicately colored
rhinestone basins

Limestones dissolve in water
deep beneath the surface
your curved artesian
demilune force

until, Amazing Prophesy! Globe of Earth
I am the geyser
hurling columns of boiling water
hundreds of feet into the air.

10. Dream: Night Outlaw

"I kissed goodbye the howling beast
On the borderline which separated you from me."

*Like a honkytonk piano walking, banjos and tamborines jangling,
drums and piano pounding, they are the showband strutting, gypsy
violins and the whole percussion section, the horns, and she is the con-
ductor, waving her arms, leading. She feels her face laughing. Her hips
and belly swinging. She paints her lips purple. She paints her nails.
She wears a dildoe and fucks the ladies and the fellows. She under-
stands for the first time that her body is flashing mirrors and rhine-
stone jewelry and more shockingly naked than ever before*

*He walks out for her. He parades. He presents the show. He is the per-
formance. He moves luminous, a transparent presence, through for-
bidden transformations, the outlaw, Jack of Hearts, the man that got
away, the matinee idol, sexual clownqueen. He is the taboo girl, whose
power reveals as it conceals, the actor beyond compare. Ramon*

*She is the lost moon of some forgotten planet coming around to his
orbit. She collapses in a crumpled heap at his feet, transfixed in the
divine moment, the archetypal movement of his body here on this 4 am
Los Angeles street, here between the frame of her hands, in her eyes
performing for her, the angel, terror of all history, the beautiful face of
a dark prince, his black curls, the rose-silk of his shirt, his fine, white
skin*

He dances. He swings his ass. He dances with his hands of silk on her tight hip. The room grows dark over the Pacific Ocean and all eyes see him. The clamor of their voices rise, Is he real? With the full moon on his face she sees he is the mime for the Children of Paradise. He is too beautiful. She is frightened. The penis of the Prince of Darkness cannot compare. It is beyond compare. She reaches for it. It is too heavy (too terrible, too real to hold in her hand.) He pulls her ass-down on his glowing belly and pushes it straight up through her thighs and says, See! See what it is like to have one. She looks down and sees what it is like and is insane with its burden. She cannot fathom how it is borne. "Remember," he whispers in her vulpine ear, introducing his tongue, "My name is Rainbow. Maximilian Rainbow. I'm a flower walking, a pink geranium. I am the show."

Wyoming

They crossed the Continental Divide and dropped down into the Big Hole Valley
before they got their first intimation of trouble ahead. The medicine man
Pile of Clouds *uttered a warning,* Death is on our trail.

     1. I AM
on Main Street, Cody, Wyoming
calling California

my voice
speaks in another place and time
simultaneous to my body
in Cody

and the words come back low on the hills

I heard one man say he cut out a woman's private parts
and exhibited them on a stick.
I heard of numerous instances in which men
had cut out the private parts of females
and stretched them over saddle bows
and wore them on their hats
while riding in the ranks.

and over there, Utah,
the words over there
of Chief Oury of the Utes

The oath of a woman is almost worthless
among the Indians.

     2.
When you reach me
traversing the great plains of your brotherhood
you come damned
by your Creed:

to withhold love
from your sister

     3. Centennial
What is thought in our little minds?
What is wanted in our great greed?

What really happened at the Little Big Horn?
Thomas Marquis' work was hidden in the archives for decades,
his research and testimony dropped, his book
unprintable:

his interviews with surviving Sioux warriors
who witnessed, midbattle, the soldiers killing themselves

his conclusion
that the slaughter of Custer's 213 men
was largely self-inflicted
due to a panic triggered by the stampede of horses
by the scarey guise and fearsome whoops of Sitting Bull's painted warriors
by the dread of what horrors awaited if they let themselves be captured

by the frontier slogan

When fighting Indians
keep the last bullet for yourself

   4.   What Really Happened North Up That Long River Valley?
Few of us will forget the wail of mingled grief, rage and horror which came
from the camp 500 yards below us when the Indians returned to it and recog-
nized their slaughtered warriors, women and children.

Now the car bears east
against the century's westering tide.
We climb dark broken masses
to a small dry sky, high
between summits

Behind us, hardly a century,
openings are being found

and Custer's wife, Elizabeth,
starts out that morning from the fort
to join him, he from whom
she is rarely separated

and grandmothers come into the country
sitting on bundles of pieced quilts and blankets
of their own spinning

and soldiers splash across streams
firing and clubbing
as they emerge from their tipis

babies crushed by boots and rifle butts, Joseph
racing by with Sarah in his arms

and the boy Crazy Horse sees with great lightning spears `
that are brighter than the sun, as thunders shake the earth,
these dead ones with their faces open to the storm
are his people

foetuses lying outside their mothers'
knifed-opened bellies

and the blue-painted dress
when he pulls it down from her face
is the young sister of Long Spear
her wide sleeves like flying wings pulled-up
and she is scalped in a bad place

Now when we reach for this land
we think of invasion
from Outer Space
because for so long we were
the alien inhuman invaders

It was our grandparents who did it.
Not mine, he answers. I see bodies crushed
as the van climbs a road so darkly narrow
there is not a center line.
Not mine, he says again. I begin to cry, hear my voice crack
under the native blood, a great red blanket
over the ground.

        5.   The Midnight Sun
In the late afternoon we come to the fork.
The map indicates *right.* But the roadsign instructs
the direct route is to the left.

We rise to the sky
on the mountain of the ancient Medicine Wheel,
America's Stonehenge,
whose people 10,000 years ago, on the vernal equinox
wheeled giant stones all the way up
the sunrays.

The lane turns dirt, a path for Bighorn Sheep.
We wind and slide through blocks,
through halls so narrow the sun never comes.
I remember the white buffalo
who showed the Arapaho how to climb out through the sky
when news reached them of the first settlers
coming in covered wagons.

We reach the crest at midnight.
He sleeps. I crouch over
the Big Horn Mountains. Above and beneath me
the stars are a million eyes
staring from the deep face of eternity.
Even to the Indians it is a mystery
who and how they carried the stones up here.
But when the white buffalo reached the top
they turned red all over
and their blue eyes
became marble-smooth and white.
They disappeared into the clouds
leaving a death song behind them in the wind.

And then I see, north and west across the black sea
of mountain ranges, floating in the lap of one,
a single, gold-chartreuse valley.
The distant round is so gold in the black
I can see granite from grass, river from road.

The Midnight Sun! Montana! The Valley
of the Little Big Horn!

I'm looking from night across so much space
I'm seeing before time
to the day already passed.

The midnight sun shines between my thighs
My urine sprays across the top of the world

6.   What Is This Place To Me If You Are Lost?
I touch the ground with both hands and see
a woman arched above the sun.
On her face the planets
are speared by lightning, her eyes
are black, in each a yellow sun.

On one bare shoulder hangs the rib of the moon,
on the other the constellation of the Sphinx:
Body of the Lion, Head of the Virgin.
In the center of each deep nipple
is a perfect rose.

She steps from mountain top to mountain top
to reach me.
She turns her face upon me.
Suddenly I know
the shocking zodiac.

You will recall how tribe after tribe
went deeper into the world
and now come from space
to sit out on your vast wastelands
to begin the great dance

And then she vanishes
into the valleys,
a brief blue sail on the Milky Way.

And the Tetons break and the Heart
of the land breaks, great chunks of ice.
Big Foot, frozen, half-risen, tries to climb
between earth and sky.

I see tribe after tribe
come to the frozen pile.
It settles in a moan, the faces open to the storm.
It's Christmas, the Mormon Missionaries
won't come out to bury them.

How did we do it?
How do we bear it?
How do we live now?

The last time I opened to the fuck of history
it broke me from the man I love
and the time before that
it broke me from my art.

For the fifth time in my life
I hear every astonished victim
I hear the earth crying

a highpitched wail coming like wind through the pines
I thought must be birds bending over me when I came here as a child,
a suffocating sexual weight coming like a moan from the ground
on which I first slept with my parents who told me
what happened to the people who belong here

and when second I heard the earth crying
my own child came from me screaming
every possible death
and with him
the Holocaust
and the South I then walked to

and when third
I heard the earth crying
Viet Nam

I took a vow
never to be a poet

I took a vow never to be a poet
because I was taught the law and order of poetry
and saw my brother become a killer
as he obeyed the law and order of the Army.
I was taught the words of a woman
are almost worthless.

I took a vow never to be a poet
because art I was taught
is too delicate to sing of genocide.
But what else could I sing
while people were being murdered
in my name?

I hear the dead in Earth.
Their songs and stories cry to me
beyond all notions of Art and Form,
the poem as museum piece
where words are molded like human skin to shade the light
like special collections
of goldfilled teeth.

But in my perfect silence,
my own unconscious fascism,
I began to die.
I was a woman without a country, a woman without words.
And with me, dying, my generation, overcome with despair.
We knew sorrow in a country words cannot enter, sorow
like a well cored through the earth.
And Demeter again sat over the hole
crying for her daughter
so loved by Death.
All the earth began to die,
the years too deadly for words,
too masculine for the feminine.

Until one Vermont winter morning
I read the Russian Ahkmatova
the poet who saw everything,
her husband at the firing squad,
her people, lovers and poets,
her whole generation destroyed,
her son in prison for her poetry
which she burned, after committing
to heart every word

who once wrote

No, not me, someone else's wound
I could never have borne it

but who, when the woman in the Siberian prison line
recognized her and whispered

Can you describe this?

gave the miraculous answer

Yes. I can.

Until I knew, as Rilke insists
is the first discovery to make
if one is to be a poet:
I will die if I don't write,
a discovery that cut through
all notions of Art,
of form, vision, communication,
occupation, money, or role in life.

Colors, Goethe said, are the suffering of the light.
And craft, I have learned, is spiritual,
the moment Orpheus steps to earth
bringing his dead love back
as song

Until I understood
years in my wild places
writing is a physical act, erotic and dangerous,
the lowering of the self
into a well almost too deep.
I must bring up the words
or perish from their rot
left inside

until I understood
that the true law and order
is cosmo logic, astro logic, geo logic,
geo graphic, organic and political
and the poetry I had been taught
was politics, lies
about indivisible united states
fictionally unionized, lies
about war between the fascist polarities
of vision and technique, of good and evil,
of woman and man, of now and then, of mine and yours,
of nature and man, of life and death,
of the physical and spiritual,
of race against race

fictions made up
to lead the mind
into murder
in the name of
what God, what happened, what thing

7.
She comes across the top of the world
She lays her hands upon me

You were born as the sun set
which is why you cannot sleep.
Day and night, you awoke to both.
You saw first the consumed heart,
the setting sun, half-earth, half sky,
the necessity to live in the present
to keep half of life
flesh-open
towards the other half
wound-closed

You were born the moment Orpheus steps to Earth
bringing his love back with him as song

But you must recall
Orpheus loved the dead too much

looked back and learned

the Dead can't be brought
onto the living Earth

To bring the song out of the blood that soaks the ground
you must remember there will be light even at midnight

You must make it living
for the Dead who do not forget the living

but livable

for the four infants found alive at Wounded Knee
wrapped in the shawls of their frozen mothers

8. SPELL FROM THE TOP OF THE WORLD INVOLVING THE
   LAYING ON OF HANDS,
   The Song of Earth Crying, The Song of Every Broken Body,
   The Song of Midnight Between My Thighs, Our Human Water,
   and I will come the long journey from Hell

Midnight lit some squaw's spray
our human water
across the top of the world.
She laid her hands upon the mountains and the plains.
She shouted this spell upon it

BREAK OPEN!

you pales with your water hearts
drag all the lakes for my body

Break open!
the deep fissures in earth
where the buried strangers
are withered hearts in a strange land

Break open your hearts
Turn around and go back
across the wintery land
Break open your hearts!
Be the opening of the Continent,
all the widest, open, already occuring world
for me to pass into

This hurt has to do with you.
It is deep. It is almost too deep.
Touch it. Touch me.
Find the wound, this
land

9. *The Linga Sharira*
And then the Scorpion curls its perfect and beautiful
deadly stinger in the dark south
the single house of Life and Death

and all our history
from which the solar body flees

shines its light through the Archer
that near-triumphant human
half-beast, half-God

before vanishing into the milky
long body of the dream

10.   I Ride The Night Filled With Space And Time
I drive us down under the Fish rising over South Dakota.
Jupiter crackles in red lightning like a neon heart.
In Sheridan I drink coffee and ache after two lovers at the counter.
I play cowboy music on the juke box, *o, take me in your arms
the way you used to*
under a sign that reads
A Sinner Is An Angel Who Slipped And Fell

I drive a narrow road across a flat land while he sleeps.
I drive a narrow hand across the Four Corners of the World,
a quivering finger beneath the Black Hills that glow,
to the geographical center of the continent.
I drive down ravines in the Pisces light
I rise over mountains aching in light
I catch in the window white juices that leak and spread from the moon
I see on the wind the stories coming in
I drive over couples fucking beneath the ground
        who turn as I turn in the winds and the rains
        who dance as I dance in the history of dung
    ·   who love as I love in their skin from the stars.
I cup and I hold them, my hands on their hips, my mouth slips along
the moonlit plateau
to the deep root that pumps
the rhythm of the range
in the exquisite precision,
the dissolution of time.

When I stop and get out
I dance around the dark hulks of diesels that drone through the night.
I bless the sleep of tired workers within, *o, blessed
be us angels who slipped here.*
I lie down on the highway.
The wind blows across the plateau of my skin.
I turn alive beneath the sky alive with animals
who whisper their stories in my ears
and finger me so lightly and forever   my belly   my throat
the small of my back
I hold so still I begin to leak beneath the white juices that leak from the moon
I hold so still the tight deep bud of earth comes slowly open like a rose
and I enter its dark tips, o play
play my body with your bow
blow your breath upon me
form me to every valley
fill me with every tree
lay me down along the waters of time, find me
o word in the river, tell me
o world in the leaves, finger
my story
deeply untold.

Infant Found Alive At Wounded Knee

1.

Something lifts me from her
once a warm bath I lay in,
now, who shudders in a great blow
that goes through me, then grows cold.

The white river I suck from her
turns to red, bitter blood.
A heavy snow begins to fall.

Under the blue starlit tepee of night
I can see them
beneath the drifting snow,
huddled heaps, scattered bundles and clots.

When the sun returns
ice slashes me like knives
glistening red
in the morning light.

The wind comes up and I become
a frozen knot
that will never be untied.

2.

I ride in his arm on horseback
across the blinding world.
He is a man who sees things
that makes his body shudder
worse than hers.
He cries *wounded,* our knees
are gone now. His tears
fall on me, a warm thaw.

Later he says
Open your mouth.
We have no choice.
I will let down the milk for you
frozen in the father river
of my breasts. What we are
is what we are. Why else
would I have them?

I name you
Little Mocking Bird
for life.

Crazy Horse

1.

I dream he is my lover.
We lie on the hard ground, beneath a single robe, the marriage blanket.
We lie against an old wooden fort on the dark prairie.
Inside, men drink as in a lighted bar.
Across the black night I feel the others, pressing in on us.
Against the black night I feel him beside me, hard and lean.
Then I feel him out there, coming, naked on his horse.

2.

In my oldest dream on earth I am shooting and shooting.
The small revolver blooms into red-hot and yellow flames
that disappear from me across the ravished nightland.
When he is beside me, dark and lean, he shows me how to shoot
to save his life. There are times when I am alone and know
he is trying to come to me out of the black night.
I hold off the others who crawl across the field to kill us.

1.

He is not like any man I have known.
He takes me all the way into the male world.
There is no separation as with other men with women.
Our survival depends on each other.
We are deep sexual mates in the physical eternity.
He is the one I have waited for, my strange,
familiar Oglala.

2.

I'm shooting into the night as they crawl across the field
to kill us. I seek him among the rifles.
When the black fog lifts, I see him afoot, surrounded.
I pull him on the back of my horse and zigzag back
through the soldiers, the burning-red bullets.

1.

Beneath the black marriage shawl, our clear bodies lie naked on the ground.
We are invisible. I braid grass stems into his light hair.
There are streakings all about us, arrows and lead balls,
but they disappear before hitting us. The danger is great
only if we fail each other. Through the whole night
a chorus of wolves resound from the frozen mountains around us.
Beneath our massive robe we lie in the deep ease of each's body.
The dark. And the dark ground.

2.

On the Holy Road he has left sticks pointing in the direction he has gone.
There I find him on the ridge above the dwindling buffalo herd,
his gun silent across his knees, watching, as if he is herding his cattle.

When he sees me coming up the long hill our eyes lock.
Behind him the storm cloud of night rolls, and thunder stirs the hair
about his waist. He starts toward me well-foward on his horse
whose neck is high, whose feet move freely. I see the splattering
of hail spots on his naked body that makes him invisible to the others.
Only the hair about his waist and the heel fringes of his moccasins
stir as he rides to me.

1.

He takes the rope of the horse from my hand
and swings his blanket about me, holding me in its folds.
He presses the wet zigzag lightning of his face against my cheek.
I put my hand beneath his large testicles. I hold him.

We lean against the hard lean night, the enemy shadows all around us.
He is the first man who lets me love him as deeply as I know.
We lie on our sides facing each other beneath the heavy black shawl.
Our heads almost touch the unpainted building of the prairie.
In this way we join our bodies. There is no separation.
With my free hand I play with the small, brown stone behind his ear.

He lies in me long, searching quietly, as with a free hand, a deep and great place.
I stir on him slowly, rising upwards, as through a flood.
He becomes a part of what is there, a hard, gold depth.
Behind his face the small red-hawk flies, making his killy-killy crying.
Without quickening his pace, moving deeply, deliberately, he listens,
he waits as I come to save his life. Only I can take this death from him,
this violet-dark son who has been killed and shines no more.
My crazy Oglala, my strange animal.

2.

He comes out of the dark purple night, naked on his horse
but for the splattering of painted hailstones, the lightning streak down his face.
As he comes he fires the prairie, burning the grass the soldier's horses
need to live, filling every clear day with great rolling clouds of smoke,
the sun, blood-red, the nightsky shining as from northernlights.
I will grieve through seven generations for this sexual lover,
this sleeper on the ground. The nightearth beneath me is his body.
I cannot answer all the bright heat of the sun, most men
with their inward meanness.
He is the strange, heavy man who goes with me.
When we lie together on the ground
I am careful not to hold his arms down.

Sleeping On Main Street In A Wyoming-South Dakota Border Town
(The Terrible Street We Have Walked In Countless Dreams)

You must find your way around the town
which has built the people's stories
into massive roadblocks.
The news is of a missing teenage boy
and the fire he has set
in your belly. You hear the people
walking above you
asleep here on their Main Street.

You walk around the forms of upthrusted asphalt.
His crying comes from every geography.
A large unknown animal
eats around the hole of your life.
Wyoming grinds under you, this ambulance
that carries you.

You are walking away. But when the boy
is found you go back.
They carry him out on a stretcher
from a tower apartment where he has been kept
unattended too long. His parents,
an old couple who have lived here
all their lives, cry and wring their hands,
ashamed.

Awake. In the street a Mennonite man
and seven young boys in pastel shirts, suspenders,
walk toward you. In the window, you turn and see
yourself, bereaved, the boy you search for, a mannequin
sending his purple rays out into the morning,
his perfect small hands into the small town
of your heart.

Sitting Bull Must Have Been A Taurus

1.

He was the only son of the Hunkpapa warrior
Returns-Again
who must have been a Scorpio
with a name like *Returns-Again*

who mounts the sky
to reveal the astounding stinger

to the Bull's face
looking, wide and open,
down upon the earth

Returns-Again was a mystic
who must have looked
to the opposite side of the universe
to the largest constellation
to name his infant son
so deliberate and large in his ways
Slow

2.

His people observed he was like a buffalo,
headstrong and fearless, opinionated,
incapable of surrender. In short, bullheaded.
In a winter blizzard buffalo never turn tail.
They face the gale and plow ahead.

As a very young man Slow
was leader of the Strong Hearts.
During battle he chose a point
in the midst of the melee
and pinned one end of a long red sash
to his heart
and the other end to the ground.
He would not retreat
unless another Strong Heart released him.

3.

Slow was not handsome but women liked him.
Courteous and gentle, like the Taurus
he must have been, those great lovers
known for endurance and fertility
he married nine times.

The first human he killed was a woman.
He was seventeen, she was a Crow,
a captive taken in a raid,
to be adopted by the tribe.
But the Crows were despised for their loose morality.
Crow men were often heard crying
across the plains as loud as women for their dead.

The Hunkpapa women concluded she was a whore.
They lashed her to a pine tree, heaped brush
around her, set it afire.
Before the flames could reach her, Slow,
who must have been ruled by Venus,
who must have pondered that this be in the stars,
fitted an arrow to his bow
and singing the song of Mercy
killed the woman suspected
of too much love.

        4.
Taurus is Spring's second chance,
the Angel of this Realm who takes rootgrip
of Aries' mindless, heartless, burning toward Heaven
and blooms it
into pulsing matter,
the Golden Calf.

Taurus is the most sensuous of signs.
Sitting Bull said to a Senate Investigative Committee

My heart is red and sweet
and I know it is sweet because
whatever passes near me
puts out its tongue to me.

Then he added to the Senators
in perfect Taurean humility

and yet you men have come here to talk to me
and do not know who I am.
I want to tell you
if the Great Spirit has chosen anyone
to be chief of this country
it is myself.

        5.
Sitting Bull learned to read and write.
Typical of the earth native, he loved
newspapers, the stories of the people
everyday around the earth.

In Lakota there are many ways to sit,
many words to describe the many states of sitting.
IYOTAKA means *sitting sacredly.*
Bull in Lakota means *Father.*

Father Sitting Sacredly
learned to write with a lead bullet
and his signature was

the head of a man
who held in his mouth
a line to a buffalo
floating in the air behind him
on its haunches, holding
the line to the man's mouth
in its hooves.

6.

Taureans are slow to anger
but when they do get mad
it is said to be the greatest anger.
They can destroy everything in their path
up to and including Scorpios.

The Battle of the Little Big Horn
was a rare day
when Sitting Bull got mad.

7.

Venus rules show business. Near the end
of his warrior life, Sitting Bull
joined Buffalo Bill's Wild West Show.
He went to Europe. But there, the faithful native declared,
It is not good for my people
for me to be parading around like this.

8.

Taureans love the land
and are possessive of what they love.
Sitting Bull led his people to Canada
in order to be free.
But the native, the maker of roots,
loves his own country, is loyal
to the risk of death.
Taurus is the sign of the patriot,
thought by many
to be a sign of stupidity. Many
do not understand Love.

A buffalo told him to return.
She approached his fire one night and said
the whites will soon be bewitched.
Today the earth is dark, but someday
it will be luminous like the sun
from the natives buried in it
who will have transformed themselves into light
which is wisdom that will stream out into space.

9.

A meadowlark told him
A Sioux will kill you.

Many Taureans are murdered
by someone they love.
One of the mysteries of the universe
is how opposites are attracted,
this faithful native, this great lover, this Strong Heart
to suffer the worst betrayal.

In white man's world Taurus rules money.
His old friend Buffalo Bill
wanted to cash-in on the publicity
of his death. In white man's world
more Taureans are in prison than any other sign.
Sitting Bull was killed by the Sioux police
called Metal Breasts because they wore
the badge of the dollar sign.
Or was it only the initials US
overlapped one on the other?

They pulled him from his cabin at dawn
warning they would kill him if he fought.
Suddenly, stubborn like a bull,
he planted his feet on the ground
and said *I'm not going*. And then it was

the sun eclipsed and the earth opened
and in a great landwave slid over him
and the tall stems of prairie grass
at Grand River where he was born,
to which he returns again,
brushed against his eyes

and he saw what he will see
so long as the grass may grow
though the plains turn to a bowl of dust
a pale sickly child named Europa
swept-away on the back
of a sacred White Cow.

Plainsongs

1. Makoshika

In the hot dusk, the face,
saucer of new moon, splashes
in the lake of your hallucination.

In unknown firmament, in fast night sky, they wait
on the wide horizon
to meet you.

Samll caskets
standing upright. Ruins. Wind blown
shards.

In the hot dawning they wait, all day
beneath sun they wait
as you walk, immigrant, west, your oxen
too weary to pull.

Lightning strikes around and through them.
Sun sets behind them, eroded
tombs in the shadow of rock, canoe moon
rowing over them.

Crows

Crows in horsehair, Crows in
hair of the dead

Crows in vegetable growth of night, enclosed
in three-quarters night

hair   glued to the ends of their own hair,
hair wild across the fullmoon face,
the body like a robe, hair swooped up
from the feet, *huka! holy*
blanket and draped
over the crook of the arm.

and some Crows stand on the plains
waiting to meet you
in the waning moon

the black falls
like water down basalt
then out from the feet, to flood,
deep rivers of living hair,
the bad land.

2. Our Strange Son

What is soul? he asks me.
I see Black Buffalo Woman
in her elktooth dress

rows and rows of elk teeth
Crazy Horse hunted down
to make her.

157

3. Ghost Dancers
Like the writer of the last century from Norway
who worked the wheatfields of Minnesota
till he coughed blood from his lungs and was told
go home for your last months, you are dying

who rode atop the locomotive to New York
his mouth open the whole way,
who arrived in the city cured, washed clean
by the air of the land

Like the wrath of 500 women warriors of the Cheyenne
who thunder out of the Rockies
wearing our dismembered parts
as jewelry in their hair

who come in a whirlwind out of the west
who come on the wind like beating wings, like bullets lost,
who pound over the broken sons
who look up from dust through the horses' hooves
who trample down the nightmare

who use the heart to span
this brink of disaster, the whipped plains,
who trod the worn-out earth, her dark islands,
searching for the final parts
the lost clues
to free us from this history

we descend the east side
the Continental Divide.

4. Paha Sapa
Now east beneath the gaze of dead Presidents
their faces pressed into rock

East, into the spermy basin
like the Mormon Jesus
on his White Stallion
descending the Rockies
to rebuild the Whitehouse
in Missouri

Now east beneath the continent's skin
and falling light I follow you
down into the bottom of the land

the sway of the bags you carry at your thighs
my hands reach
back under the sun, the distance of history
you leap

Blondstorm, male road, white man, stoneheart
you are not easy to enter

5.   Second Wind
I am seasick on a dry land.
Sandpaper keeps throwing me back
to a rocky wall.

At night, beached by the side of the road,
I burn the parts of you,
my fires by buffalo dung.
The flames lap against the wall.

I come upon women
moving out beneath the attic
of the blue sky
to mutilate the bodies
of dead soldiers

and the buffalo skulls,
bare now and bleached,
still turned toward the west,
toward the Great Sun.

6.
Mornings I wake
to speak to you
but a train of covered wagons
comes from my mouth.

We drift like mirage
east into the hot dawning
and the shadows of stiff trees.
Day takes the color
of nails and manganese.

7.
Humanity is the foreign country here.
The air carries half the country with it.
The air
is a coercion
of opinions

can turn
a flock of birds

I am seasick in these pastures of God.
Sandpaper keeps throwing me back
to the bad lands,
against the ghastly faces
preserved in mountain.

8. Chippewa Dream Song of Thunder
Sometimes
I go about pitying
myself
while I am carried by the wind
across the sky.

9. Immigrant's Song
You rumor your blood through a sweet reed
to mine, you enter my childhood,
Blood Brother
your hands strip my face of its country,
you let fall my ghost shirt,
the rags of an old thought.

10. Passage on the Wind
The wagons tack against the wind
which slows the pull
to the coast
to meet the ones
who went by water
in the light and easy air
around the Horn.

The wheels roll over
the foreign words bounced-out,
now weeds in the plowed fields,
now voices in the air

A Lakota trades beads
for bolts of cloth.
Rides off, East,
the other way
within the Wind

40 yards of colored calico
streaming behind him

11. Plainsong
Oh, let me occupy space
without filling it

12.   Dream Song of Thunders
A mosquito flits at the window wanting in.
We laugh that *mercy* is a trucker's word.
The sun sets like your face
in the dark range of my thrust-up knees.
The sun, now the glowing red slit
you glimpse

The beating wing of night hovers
The trees nod blindly along the river bank

The sun sets
like the live coal you put in me

like the body opened and the heart exposed
too red and beating

Everything, the Sioux say, shall perish,
except your heart.

13.
Moonlight in the windows
the blanket tangled with childhood

the hood ornament: then a young stallion
led us

Moonlight on these flats, unexplored
rumors of gold.
Moonlight across his sleeping face,
across the dark herds who graze
the round belly

My head full of rolled
prairie

and the four souls of the Mandan:

a white shooting star,
a meadowlark, lightbrown, hardly visible,
the dim lights around the abandoned village,
and the fourth: *a black shadow*

14.   Prairie Rose

A rough boy presses through me,
rearranges me on a map.
His farmer hands peel my face
from husks of corn.
The tense narrow body rises
on his tense narrow body, moves me
into the farmhouse

silent in the gully, behind the windbreak

We must restore the soil, he says

I hold his child to the kitchen window
I hear my name called
way off by the river

The story forms quickly
The clouds rise in the evening sky
The winds whip the stiff cottonwoods
The rains beat the flatlands
The sun sets on the smoky hills

I only dreamed that bridge I built
across the Missouri

Hard Country

The sun crosses over the heavens and sinks below the prairie.
I walk from room to room as I have done now for a hundred years
and keep coming upon new faces that make me recall
the one I was born in. That was the winter
the snow came early and lay so deep and white
no one dared go out into the open without the face
dark-painted against the sun. Sometimes the mirror
where the hall turns will show the same red shoulders,
the same long black hair rising and falling with the motion
of horses before me, with eagle feathers in every mane and tail,
and beyond, a wide extent of desolate prairie, over which
little parties of naked horsemen are rapidly passing,
who vanish then suddenly from sight, as if
diving into the earth.

I rarely come to this room without the acrid smell of him rising to me.
Many times I've thrown open all the windows to air the room.
I'll think he's gone. Then one day I'll climb the stairs to his door
and smell him in there and remember how I lay with him those nights
moving my mouth over his back.

Each night the sun slides out below the clouds
and lights a section of the rainbow that feels like solid
air around me when I lean back into my chair.
If I could tell you what I see in the light then when it strikes,
or in the center of the tornado when it sets down,
or in the mirror in that unearthly moment, before the vacuum
swallows up everything from the past and the future, and they come....
Well, they come. Ghosts. All around me, as far across
the burning prairie as I can see.

When I was a girl I saw them doing the ghost dance, their faces
painted scarlet-red, circling and circling backward against the clock,
people who are opposite, moving to the left, as in the Bible
or somewhere I read that the world is a double movement,
the movement to the right, adding up and expanding,
as times goes on and determining events that are passing.
And the other to the left, a backward dance,
folding up and contracting as times goes on, through which
the seeds of the future take form. It is said if you know
this movement you know the future, like the cottonwood
contracting into a seed that is shaped like a star
and then the future unfolding of the seed
into a tree.

When they danced something happened to the earth.
One said you think you're just surrounded by your tall buildings
and farms, but we're all around you. You'll never be rid of us.
It happens mostly at twilight and grows into a large violet shape
that goes on and on behind the tree and the birds sitting on the wire
like the old men at the drugstore counter gossiping. Sometimes
I can see the boys I used to know staring through their faces
like Miss Campbell's lesson about the hoards of Mongolians coming
down from the North, conquering the Chinese, slaughtering

and butchering and destroying everything. The Chinese
with their 5000 year old history were unprepared for such people.
They were simple keepers of the land, they'd always lived there.
And in three generations, there were no Mongolians.
They'd all become Chinese. She always said to us
when you want to remember a story of the losers winning
remember the Mongolians and how they lost themselves
in the Chinese they destroyed because the land itself
is Chinese. As here, the 4th of July has always been
their holiday. I heard Pa say to that Strong Heart, see
you Indians recognize the United States, you celebrate
the 4th of July. The Strong Heart looked at him the way they do
and said, you recognize us. You chose our day
for your country's birthday. You don't understand
the forces you're fighting in a land that's foreign to you.

I shut my eyes and listen to the cottonwood branch scrape
against the roof, crying like a fiddle without breath.
In the past I would have cut the branch
before it tore the roof. Now I think to let things
happen as they will, like the floor sloping,
the foundation going bad. I shut my eyes and see
the covered wagons coming, covering everything, hoards of immigrants
coming out of the East with the dream of owning their own land,
making it as they want, the men on tractors and big semis
and I feel myself floating out in the air ahead of them
and see them being swallowed up, one by one, in a cloud
like the cloud that swept up Custer's men, clouds of alkali,
dust and gunsmoke rising in a circle of heat all around them,
making a darkness as of evening. All our stealing and killing.
They're inside our bodies now where they can't be fought.

The storms in the west shine through the holes
in the lace curtains Mother hung before she left.
They've grown thin now, their weight pulling
the little holes larger all the time. The wishbones
are still here in the window I wouldn't let Brother pull apart.
Even then I knew the knots in the walls to be galaxies
they come through at night, strange spirits from other worlds
who say to me soon there'll be no white people.
White people are bewitched and don't see what's been going on
these hundred years they've been dancing. Just as Old Weather Woman
said to me when I was a girl, *The people who follow the buffalo
eat well while those who chase the whites are like
the ones who chase the rabbit. Even while they eat
they are hungry.* And so they just quit messing with us.

As Mother did when she left us to go to those people
leaving a note on the kitchen sink addressed to father
and the brothers, addressed to their Silence, she said
and their huge hands forever spilling seed to the ground.
She just up and went to the I AM people who believe in flying saucers
when they were forming their commune on Camas Prairie.
That was sixty years ago. Now no one knows who their father is,
who the grandfathers are. They meet out on the plains
and talk with the aliens and chant I AM, I AM.

And the men went on plowing, never saying a word about her,
plowing so many years I began to feel sorry for the earth.
She said I would feel her absence for a long time
then I would know her again. Before she left
she read me a story by a mystery writer
The Day The Earth Screamed about men who wanted to dig
through the earth. They dug and dug. They came to a place
deep inside her that looked strange. When they touched it
with their digging machines, she screamed.

I can't tell where they come from, from deep in the earth
or from outside our realm. They say when white people die
they go to other planets, but they stay here
because this is their planet. Nights the windmill cranks and cries
a whanging, screeching rust music that sounds like
lost souls calling over the dismal town, like
a great keening gone up. Sometimes when I'm out there
flying ahead of myself through the clear and beautiful air
the whole calvacade will sweep by me in a moment,
the women in their gaudy ornaments tinkling as they ride,
the men whooping, laughing, and lashing forward their horses.
I see everything in the living light then
and I see the earth is changing, the weather so unpredictable now,
no one understands, she's changing her consciousness
in order to save herself. They tell me she's a very old soul
who has incarnated this time as a planet. Sometimes
I can hear her crying of the white people, her face
dark-painted against the sun.

I was born in this house and know I am dreaming of my death,
the way the sound of the highway enters me
like the distant singing when you think it's the blood inside your ear,
or an urge to go look at the plain,
your back to the town and Corn Palace.
In bed it is as if I lie down with the mountains
moving my mouth over a flood plain where the river curves
through the buttes and I forget who I am.

They say a drowning person sees her whole life pass in front of her.
Now I see my whole life passing in front of me
and I see they've always been here. Carrying on around me.
I can see them so clearly, coming on the red road.

Detroit I

We spend the day in his uncle's house
looking at old photographs.
We keep our legs folded beneath the plastic couch
so the family can get by.
His uncle studies each page with me
as if he too has never seen
those times, these women. He says
with interest, not quite a question,
this has been my life.

In the old black and whites they come up from the South.
For work. The daughters come, then grow
into the bright toothy years. Then leave
in small ceremony, Southern Baptist
converted Catholic.

Here he is a sailor in Long Beach, the sailor
I loved when I was too young. We ate in the car
outside Shrimpy Joe's, watched the tattoo artists
work their parlors, the sailor faces turning white.
The naked woman he loved so much
he suffered her image to be burned into his flesh
grows old now on his arm. He remembers the screams
from the roller coaster, and the fog:
Hung out there behind the breaker wall.
You couldn't tell your own ship.

His irony humors the poor domesticity.
His jokes fart his poor masculinity.
My girls, he says to the photos, *my own*
flesh and blood. Once he was a man
I could have married. *Ten years,* he keeps saying,
then I'm going home.
Now I'm ashamed.
This exile. This work. This wait
for your life to be over.

His oldest daughter rents the house next door.
Comes over, tired, pregnant, her third
in three years. Her husband, wired on speed,
called *Skinenbones,* hauls trucks
to St. Paul. Calls him *Pa.*

The teenage girls from the neighborhood
and the last daughter, fifteen,
troop through to see
the dark, orphan cousin.
The sexy, middle girl who looks like him
sits on the floor in the corner, refusing to talk.
She's the one we always thought
looks most like your mother.

There are no wedding pictures
of the one who looks like the one
who threw herself in the lake.
But she lives over on Joy Road
in a trailer they bought for her
and her two year old son.

His wife, Aunt Eula Lee, is dying,
a slow invasion of the blood
they can't stop. Everyone
praises her cheeriness. *Seems like no time
since we got here,* she says, serving us
chicken and dumplings. *But I'm not going back.
I want to be buried where my daughters live.*

I lay my book down before his mother
who stares into this cramped life
from some cherry blossom time in the old hills
before she went mad, walked into the lake.
I dream I'm trapped in a phone booth
trying to call my father in the West.
I'm screaming about a man with Detroit
tattooed on his face. The needles
suck blood, inject children
goosestepping in place.

Then I hear him downstairs
getting up from his wife.
He packs the lunch pail, runs the bath.
He leaves through the garage door,
taking slippery possession of the night
he's paid to maintain. I would have even
loved his name

Boyd Adams is an Oiler.
He'll get to work the day shift
the year he retires.
He's been on the list
since his first week in '54.

Detroit II

Huron

In the month of the snapping trees
when the sun descends, I am chosen
the male block out of which
they will carve their woman.

They touch me with their clubs and firebrands,
drive me inside
to the unknown passion.

My limbs and penis are thrown
upon the plain.
I am opened and burned soft,
my flesh slit into the woman's wound,
a thousand clitorises cut loose.

They are good lovers. They touch me deep
but I do not die.
Now another
sleeps with my wife.

I am kept alive for the sun to rise
so I can sing to Him
the Song of Woman.

I am brought back from the dead as woman
for the sun to see.

Late Summer '42

The boy and I crossed the Ohio, late summer, '42.
I was sick with morning.

I was sick with the cruel and perfect
Lords of Tennessee. Before they could know
their son was the father, I fled.
He had forced himself into me
and he would have taken the child from me,
Johnny, swinging just two months
between my hips.

We came to the Ohio, the bridge
from my dead and imperfect mother.
The sun was leading me from morning
and all I couldn't stomach.
I was sick with property, propriety, money.
I was desperate, we *hitchhiked, any* means
to escape
like Eliza and her son
who escaped the bloodhounds
by crossing the Ohio
on cakes of ice.

Our ride, a nice man, would have taken us
deep into Indiana. It was getting dark.
We had no place to stay.
Still, we got out
at the Cincinnati Bridge.
I took the two year old in hand
the man now that you love,the boy
I can't remember birthing, things
were that bad, and we walked
across the Ohio

so through the California childhood
without history or bloodroot
I could tell them our story began
when we walked across the Ohio

and went out west where we'd never be found,
like my great grandfather
who fought for the North when he was thirteen
and then fled Memphis, crossing the Mississippi
to homestead the wilderness.

Kentucky: A Cherokee Name of Magic

Down in the hollows, down in the blue
stories, barns smothered in kudsu
like striking miners beat into the dark
and bloody ground

Like settlers sifting across Appalachia,
like a deer suddenly from woods,
a barefoot woman in a yellow bonnet
crosses the Interstate in front of us.
A white plastic purse dangles from her arm
onto the hills

the path for eons to her old Kentucky home.
She crosses the new Four-lane to Mama's
needing a roadsign: *People Crossing*

The road we always took
over the hot backyards of Lexington,
the barelegged women seated under their clotheslines
and babies crawling under the sheets, around Mama's
gossip, her blueveined, blue
thighs, her whispers

of good story, her gospel, as God's spell
I read my mother's suicide note,
the last thing she said to my dad was
I'll see you in heaven, there's where

my heart is turning
across the Kentucky, deeper
into screaming katydids, mimosa, the bridge so high
we get out to see
the old highway below he took as a boy

to his half-brother, the road we take now
to his first model of a man,
who says any fool knew
but the slide-rule boys
the banks were gonna cave,
to all that's left of the good blood,
the pillared porch where once the slaves helped out
and his wife's
self-made, pretty highstrung
face, *oh, honey,*
I just got to get out tonight

takes us to dinner on Daniel Boone's path
tells us

a teenage girl down there
drowning as we pass over
the Kentucky
south on the Wilderness Trail

Tennessee

Until they came/and trance-planted, touched/as they were by such goings-on

1.
We shall always be arriving
at the strange shores
where we first began

because the earth turns
and returns to those places
that remember us
in the moment of our births

because the earth is round
but we did not know this
the first time around

2.
And when they came again to the strange shores
and set about the Clearing

referred to by late historians as

the Vanguard of Civilization
the Rearguard of the Revolution

the first real Americans
the children of the woods
over-the-mountain men
a peculiar breed of men
a criminal element, but mostly
those without means

her transmontane citizens

3.   Cismontane
When the strange lands had been cleared
the years of quest and toil had seared the genes
with a dream of hunger and greener grass
so that nights in the clearings
along the eastern rivers, the stories and rumors
ploughed the trackless forest
west through the low river gaps.

How far does the world extend?
At night you can hear the voices
west of the Great Barrier.
In the day someone walking in the woods

Often I wake in the fields
to the setting sun
and wonder how far the world extends.

4.

The Visit in 1673 By The First Anglo Saxons To Set Foot On The Soil of Tennessee

They entered by way of the Nolichucky Valley
Of the two

one was killed by Indian John
who
    ript open his body
    drew out his hart
    and held it up in his hand

    5.

    1730

What had he ever known
in the dark forested valleys
of the western flowing streams

of royal transactions in London

And so they went to the strange shores
to the place called England
The Great Chiefs of the Cherokee Nation
Attakullakulla, the Little Carpenter, and Oconostota

so that even forty years later
when they came up again for the last time
The Great Warrior Path
as old men leading their young
to rid their nation forever of the British
he had a dream that night
in which the Red Coats pinned him down
and shot images of a far eastern city,
its dirty streets and its sorrows,
into the balls of his eyes

Looking For The Melungeon

In a past life, Love
we crossed the sea in a great wave
before it was uprooted

Through dreams of water and former cities
we came

settled these parts
with mountains running up like walls,
passes to valleys
leading nowhere.
We told
no outlanders
our tales.

Your hand touched the night.
I parted the darkness.
Our great blood circulated round
a Blond's face.
Our legends scattered the Jews'
lost colony.

Now we're full of strangers,
shipwrecked Portuguese,
blue-eyed Indians whose ancestors
talked in books.

Somewhere south of here, divers search
for the body. Cold, dumb fish. We could be
Japanese.

Talking Melungeon. Appalachian
African. Mountain-locked migration.
Unknown. Song sung.
Way low

Take your mind
clean away.

At Cumberland Gap Post Office A Letter From Loretta in Los Angeles

Blue has become
an important color to me
now that my mother is dying

I look up to the dark soil of the Blue Ridge
that lies on top of his mother
and write her

I have heard it is an old custom
in these hills
people place trout ponds
on the graves of their loved ones
with the inscription

A Blue Blanket To Warm You

Great Smoky

1.

Walking down the street alone
statues in front of the courthouse
tops of their heads
turning blue

In the store windows
Women Who Spied
Rickety neon, old roads
leading out, reaching
down
the boondocks

Dogwalk   Rock Batter   Mohawk

Crooked backstreets, eyes on me,
old merchants, arms crossed
in the crisscrossed neon
in doorways, their tongues
up my legs, the tongues
of different times

Tusculum   Afton   Romeo

Walking down the street
by his side
Two days he hasn't talked
Statue in front of the post office:
the way they think he died

2.

Where the three come together
my uncle pointed
when he came down to meet us
on the edge
of the Great Smoky

Took apart, then put together
this old cabin
1700s
Numbered every log, carried it
up here

On the shelves
Ghosts of the Cumberland
Deathlore in the Kentucky Foothills

Your grandfolks lived awhile in Afton.
When the strikes finally ended
he was too old to work.

He tells me of his mother. My grandmother.
He has letters from her brother in Memphis.
Biggest hands on any man I ever saw.
He addressed her different ways,
Lura, Maude, Sister, and in some,
Sweetheart

3.   Bloodlines That Have Been Lost
From behind, from over these mountains, to wake
in the middle of the night
beneath this smoky mountain
peaked attic, *diaphragm not in*, it doesn't matter
first time ever with him like this, moving around
on me, behind me, inside me, trying
on this feather bed
to piece together
our history
what is always missing
the genital members, trying
to reconstruct them
in our image, fitting

to conceive
a ghost
from Tennessee
from whence we both
come

The quiet dignity
of my aunt and uncle
in the next room

Down crooked stairs, 1700s
creaky, dark, *I have to*
I tell you, if only I could tell you
I have to

Searching for the light, out
into the night, barefoot, naked
Deer over there, *don't tell anyone*
there's wild turkey here

4.   deathlore
On the bathroom floor downstairs
legs high on the wall, dim
pioneer antiques, pray
it's not too late, pray
the poison kills the Tennessee sperm.
Always pray
it doesn't kill you too.

In the dark bathroom, head in your lap,
crying, *if only*
I could tell you

Comfort Me With Apples, Stay Me With Flagons, Jesus, Lover of My Soul,
Let Me To Thy Bosom Fly

     1.   Knoxville
The Tennessee River flows by my bed.
In the morning I walk the city asking
in which direction it flows.
No one knows.

Today is election day.
Alcohol will not be sold
until the polls close.

The sheriffs are running

On every corner the words scream
BLACK WOMAN RAPED IN '63
BY COCHRAN, favorite son

Two policemen took me out
to an East Knoxville rock quarry.
Cochran raped me in the backseat.
The other policeman only acted
like he was having intercourse.

     2.   Back Into Landscape
A *package store,* he says, *so familiar,*
this rain in summer, this song from Nashville,
take my hand and pull me down, I'm easy,
it's called
I'm easy

This cloudburst in Knoxville,
this getting off work, this rain
and neon in the darkening sky, this
Tennessee Waltz, this beat of the heart,
this Cherokee drama, this Trail of Tears
unto the hills

this kudsu
legend says you better close your window
nights to keep it out, these layers,
this smoke rising,
this cauldron green.
The sky is silver, the road ahead
the road behind
breathes these clouds, this road
the slow transformer, the smoke of Tennessee

this backroad,
this bleached blonde bent double in her milkshed
this drive-up window, this booze
sold illegally

these two pillars, antebellum
these white marble stairs

this couple sitting on what used to be
their front porch, all
they got left now
after
the fire, this tent outside Bristol
this Old Fashion Revival
by Willard Tallman

Tired of Crying on God's Shoulders?
Try leaning
in his everlasting arms

Billy Graham
summer nights, his tent
down the tracks, across
the coal field, Industrial,
late 40s voice of god

even in my bed, midnight
I could hear him scream
God's body got soul!

Now you drive me
Nolichucky backroad, Church of the Cherokee,
mailbox, barnslope, Bible Belt,
coming into Deep Gap, Blowing Rock,
Mouth of Wilson,
Hitchhiker says
this hyar road
the windiest road
Southwest Virginia's got

letting the boy off, the world
goes on without you, canebreak, cabin creeks,
covered bridge, it doesn't matter
walking into these woods, your genes
winding through all this funk,
gullywasher, rusted
mobilehome down in hollarslide, scattered parts
of cars parts, hanged black men
across the Cumberland.

      3.   Lone Mountain
We stand around his Pa's old store,
end of the road, stoned.
We stand around the stares, *who*
Who? Thinks he's been around
bringing her here.

Used to go with my Pa way back there
pick up folks in his truck
so they could shop.
Only way most could get here.
It's a strange place, man, you have no idea.

Same old man as a kid, chew
Big Blue Lick, hours, years,
reading comic books, turn to stone

Did alot of Christmas shopping here,
Middlesboro, Kentucky
if we couldn't get to Knoxville,
snow and stuff.
There's the clinic my mother was in.
I can remember her arms all black and blue
where they gave her the shots.

Lived here awhile after she was gone.
Civil War Hospital.
We found handcuffs, leg chains
in the basement.

This is where Ila May Johnson lived.
Told you about her, lives in Baldwin Hills now, L.A.
You can see why she left, she
hated it here.

Gumming apple tobacco. Years, the emptying hills.
Now like everywhere, new houses
slow filling.

                4.
I sit the shadow-racing afternoon
on the stone bench his mother sits on
in the photo he carries in his pocket
just before she drowned.

Ruth, his stepmother
comes home from Knoxville
where she goes to get her vodka

The house, a dark underground, a cave.
Knicknacks, whatnots, antiques, old store signs.
She always did keep
curtains, blinds, everything
pulled.

Don't come near my pickles
in the kitchen, dearie,
if you're menstruating.
Did you hear, son,
Wayling next door
shot hisself.

The boys come over, drink mountain dew, play
poker, poke fun. *Did you hear?*
Jesse Lynn, he felt the callin a few years back
after the weddin, took up the ministry,
witnessed the power in Lonesome Valley
served as the Body
of Christ.

Chewing chewing tobacco.
Did you hear, Saturday night,
those two Tazewell boys
lay theirselves down middle of the road
fell asleep, somethin, no one knows,
Run right over, sometime,
middle of the night.

Gumming apple tobacco

    5.   Appalache
People come
undone

So much beauty
is violence to the soul
and the body
which is delicate

People can't think

what to do

Going Around The Country Looking For Your Mother

1.

To get to this part of Tennessee
the road goes first up
over the saddle
out of Tennessee
onto the dark and bloody ground
Kentucky
then east into the crimped Virginia corner
then down into Lonesome Valley

where on the Tennessee line
at Snake Hollar
the road turns dirt

and the sign says
When Daniel Boone
returned here the following spring
he found the bodies of his two young sons
disinterred
by wild animals.

Now a tobacco patch is wild
with hairy wings
flying green about the foamy heads
of two black men
who bend and rise
to cut.

A heavy female arm
pulls back the curtain
of her mobile home
as we come down the road.

He stops at the corner grocery to ask
where we are.
A woman hurries through the jingling door
he goes through, moves quickly
across my window.
Did you see her
the blue eyes, the nappy hair?

Melungeon.
People in thse hills
don't know where
they come from.

2.   Aunt in Lonesome Valley
In an emerald hollow, in screaming catydids, down
a lapped ridgeside
we find a tall, ancient house
draped in a kudsu shawl, silver
in need of polish, adrift
a million butterflies.

Isn't this something?
I remember the place from a kid.
Ten the last time here.
She has sons my age
but I never did see them.
Uncle Boyd said whenever he'd come
they'd make it for the woods.

We inch across the rickety footbridge.
The rotted planks fall
with each step
over the moss and holes
to the tumbling creek, *eons,*
a duck down there
floating out
from under us.

The two screen doors are dark open stares.
They may be watching us.
The porch is swept away
beneath the red and yellow tulips
in the painted coffee cans.
No one comes
to either eye.

High above the roof
cows balance the blowing sky,
the too-green world.
The tobacco patch flutters and flies
its thousand flags. And butterflies
everywhere, a sister
who killed herself at 30, another
dead of cancer, two in Detroit. And red
clover, a corn patch way up there, a tire
riding a fencepost. *The neighbors,* he warns
are watching us.

As we leave
a woman is starting down through the fields.
You feel in each stringy step as she drops
her dread
what could be waiting for me
back at the house?

We have come this far; it is enough.
The road pulls us away.
At the four corners, a dirtroad cross,
the antebellum mansion
is a barn now
for tobacco.

    3.   Aunt Rema
They said I'd never walk again.
But I showed em. No. No special exercise.
Just stood up.

Even so, I lost my husband, 15th of April.
After what they did to me,
he just wouldn't go
to the hospital.

I always thought you looked like your mother,
the child most like her.
But with that beard,
hard to tell.

Your pa bought a plot
right next to her.
But your stepma
planted him somewhere else.
Never could understand that.

You don't know
what a slop pail is?
Tatter holes for storage?
Honey, are you saved?

      4.   Aunt Mary's
O, Geneva, your mother.
I took care of her, you know.
After her parents died she came here.
Poor little orphan, she was the sweetest thing.
Shy. She was always so shy.
Wouldn't do nobody no harm.

She went to work for your pa
but his mother rode her something terrible,
worse than cleaning lady.
Still, they got sweet on one another.
You know, Aunt Mary, she says to me,
we're courtin. He leaves me
notes under the pillow
for when I make up the bed.
But his mother
wouldn't have it.

Oh, she loved him.
I never saw nobody
love a man like that.
She was sick, she must have been sick.
Your grandmother in the house the whole marriage
riding her worse then cleaning lady.
She was so young.
It used to be the custom in these hills,
the men waited till their late 40s,
then married the young ones.
She was sick, no body
in their right mind, she loved
her children.

Her belly button broke-open.
During the pregnancies.
I'll whisper this, dear,
a man, not even a son,
might not understand.
It never did heal up.
She showed it to me once.
Terrible.
It was oozing out
all the time, like nothin
you ever seen.

They say she got all dressed up,
gloves and hat like she was going to church,
and just walked down the road to the lake.

It'll Be A Bad Winter If Screech Owls Sound Like Women Crying

1.   *Eighth Grade Graduation, Lone Mountain School*

Her dress is pale silk
gathered on bare shoulders.
In the hollow of her throat
one glass bead
falls from the string,
pulsates a tiny light
to pierce her high chin.
Her hair is cropped, dark and straight,
the bangs spill heavy to the eyes,
her son's eyes, *the eyes don't change,*
he says, they are deep and wide as lakes,
as tears down on some secret shore.
The corners of her mouth are expectant,
loved, resist
the man who bribes
smile.

2.   *Carnival*

She has her picture taken at the carnival.
It is 1946. *She is even more beautiful.*
She holds the man I am with now
on her lap. She holds his head up
but he moved and is a blur, *which is
significant, don't you think?*
He is the same reluctant lover,
but *she looks like a contemporary,*
he says, *like any girl
living now.*

The eyes don't change.
But the hair is longer, flies
through kinky waves, a carnival ride,
the bangs sweeping down and across
the right eye
which hides in the shadow.
She is even more beautiful, but you can tell,
he says, *she isn't loved.*
*There is the issue of murder. Occasionally
it comes up.* There will always be
the issue of the man.

3.   *Bituminous*

*He used to tell me of the hired guns
who rode the trains through the tent cities.
When the strikes ended, the men retired
behind the circles of women.
The women in these hills
are strong.*

After the mines closed
the men had nothing
but the black dust that filled their lungs
until there was no room to breathe.
It took him years to die,
a slow suffocation. Finally, I think
it was his heart.

Once I heard someone say he could have,
should have, would have
murdered her.

My father was a simple man
with desperate needs.

Song of Songs: The Lady In The Lake

(Norris Lake was the first TVA project, named for Senator Norris of Arkansas. "This is the lake, you know, my mother drowned herself in when I was ten.")

1.   Shelter Cove To Lone Mountain By Canoe, "about 25 miles."

See how the roads disappear into the water
fences, old farms, the water covered everything

Biggest fish I ever caught from that spot
Swimming
from about ten on
All my time spent here
Lived on
Eskimo pies, cokes
Sometimes I wonder
how I made it

Baptised
when I was twelve, right there
the preacher
and anybody who wanted
came down
I don't know why this place fascinated me
You could swim so deep
the fish would nibble at your feet

There's the road to our house
beneath the railroad trestle
See how it leads right into the water

Once I jumped from that trestle on a dare
Thought I'd never hit the water
Then I thought
I'd never come up

The sun is a knife on bare skin.
A fish slices the surface.
Jump in, he urges, *jump in*
So you can say
you swam in Norris Lake.

2.

She comes through the woods
on the dirt road from the house.
Her three boys play in the field.
They hardly notice when she waves goodbye.
She feels a fine elation for them, for herself,
this most perfect mother thing she does.
She wears her Sunday dress, the one she married in,
her white hat and gloves.
She has left the note on the kitchen sink.
I'll see you in heaven.

The small waves of our canoe
reach her nyloned feet, suck quickly
into the holes her high heels make,
rise up the straight seams
on the back of her calves

like the one that got away
or a fish caught
just for the sport of it
and thrown back

I'm going to the halls of water
What is air to me?
I can't breathe in it

       3.
Shock, the cold other world,
the dive to the farmer,
to her face sleeping with open eyes, *Who*
will make you fishers of men?
to the baptism at twelve
my body poured again through the white gown
by the preacher who looks like my father
who wears the tie with my name
I am the Rose of Sharon
and the lily of the valley.

With both hands I took hold
the shocking steel arm
the thick male bush on the burning flesh

to give up personal will
and follow him,
I will make you born again,
he lowered me down into the kingdom of God
to wash my sins away

leaving the congregation gathered like trees on the shoreline
and entered the silence of the other world
the silence of the father

the son, the holy ghost, the shocking
return to this eyes

the gown turned sheer in the water

the pink whorl of blossoms
when I look down
to the mark on the right one
beneath the erect nipple
where an angel kissed you, my mother always said
now taken by his eyes
seeking Revelations.

4. *"I Am Sick With Love"*
I explode from water to the light.
He laughs, his arms folded across his chest.
He won't pull me in even if I beg.
I look to the far shore, go under

Immense waves of sorrow, fear
descend with me, this water of his wrath
the world turning over and over
in its last images, the beautiful couple
on her water

the terrible body exploding without breath
the pieces flying of silver fish, drowned trees, a farmer's hand
thrashing around to grasp the men, the rapes,
the real estate deals, the constant treading
just to survive

There.   Breathe.   Air so wonderful, sky
makes you cry.
The whole world in light. My father
fishing on the banks. *Oh, Daddy, I loved you so.*
You could save me still

But she hardly hesitates on the shore beside him,
then steps in, slipping down through the last miraculous air
in her Sunday clothes, entering veiled, in prayer, the hushed
sanctuary, the green cold, her earthly dress now
dragging her the long terrible path down
through holiness and voices, through faces
lit in darkness, the terrible wrath gone over her
as her navel, at last, *O Jesus to thy bosom,* oozes her out
into the beautiful waters her sons swim in,
floating her mother's farm in golden light, in songs of the planets,
the jubilant weeds of the glory land enfolding her, a fish now
going down under the world

to the woods and meadow where she ran as a girl
that bleak day she saw, bent on the fence beneath a rainbow
her wretched and cruel father sobbing
as the senator strode across the land
a string of reporters recording with camera and pen
his dedication speech, *We'll make a great country of her yet.*

5.   A Drowning Person Sees Her Whole Life Pass Before Her:
       The Pornographer
Take me up and cast me into the sea.
I am in love with you.

I am in love with you
because of your mother.
I left my husband for your mother.
I've come all this way to find her.
She lies at the bottom of you,
the deep dark water that covers you.

How long it has taken me to understand.
When he brought you home for me to fuck,
bearded hitchhiker through Albion
on your way to somewhere else,
I said, all right, I'll drown for you.
Husband. I love you.

But when you stood over us
as he held me down
I saw someone in your eyes.
She was watching from the water.

When he was through
I took you to the bed
beneath the map. I showed you
my inability to see underwater.
You loved me for the men
I've survived by drowning.

But then the country came into me on the wind of your mouth.
I heard her crying *you can save me*
it's not too late.

Now we are here
adrift her suicide, this manmade lake,
this lake of rue, my mother
in law, the climax of our story

which began, can you believe?
on Valentine's Day.
Yes. Believe it. See now, you're rowing away
leaving me to drown
with your grandmother
you have just told me
drove your mother to it.

Your father couldn't help it.
And I am a good swimmer. Seductress
of men who hate me. From the crib
I saw him looking at me.
I planned then to be beautiful.
I saw it was my only chance.
Every man I've ever loved
has wanted to kill me.
But if I am perfect
if I am drowned
I'll be all right.

     6.   *"Before I was aware/my fancy set me in a chariot beside my prince."*
The trees rise to swallow the sun.
Then flame.
The sky is rose cumberland,
hushed striated cumulus.

You have your mother's eyes
he says across the darkening
as I row.
My mother always told me
I have my father's eyes.
As if it were her wish
that I see as he sees
and not see her.

She is hard to find.
She is the road furthest to the left,
the one that leads into the water.

The only sound is our breathing,
water's whisper along the sides.
This canoe is our ego, he says.
Down there the world empties
into the unconscious,
a heliotrope mirror.

And down there is our mother.
The oars churn her fiery water.
I tell him of sleeping on the beach
at Chappaquiddick that long night
the first men were landing on the moon,
of waking again and again
in the nightmare dunes
to her trapped in his toy car
as it fell through water.
I could hear her crying
you can save me, it's not too late.

And he tells me
near here Daniel Boone met his wife.
He was firehunting on that moonless night
stalking the forest with a blazing torch
to attract a deer
which he would shoot between the two points
of reflected firelight, its eyes.

But Rebecca was attracted to the light.
When he saw the double gleam and prepared to shoot
only an intuition he later could not understand
stayed him.   .

We eat cheese and bread.
He kneels in the canoe's rocky dance,
pees. I slip
over into her, the cold dark. Tread
the warm river.

Death, Whitman whispers, *death, death
is the sweetest, lushest word.*

7.   *"Killing is a form of our wandering mourning"*
The beautiful woman who wanders the land by day
and is the bear in heaven at night, most
conspicuous constellation, hangs
now in the cedar, *Ursa,* now as we float,
as we rise to meet her in the Gap,
now Little Bear as we spin, *Virgin,*
Sister, Psyche, Goldilocks,
letting the water take us, *Kentucky,*
Virginia, Geneva, the Arkansas senator's long finger
in the Tennesee Clinch.

He plays the harmonica. Harmonious lines of Earth.
She turns and returns you
to the place
that dreamed you.

Galactic space pours
through the pounding hooves of the Horse
into which we drift. Who will show a child
just as it is? *Who'll set her*
in her constellation and put the measure
of distance in her hand? When I was a girl
I knew God's face could not be looked at.
When I first saw the constellations
drew the unbearable story lines
of the impossible stars
I knew again self
as it is known
by galaxy and cedar cone.
I knew again soul, the Holy Breath that is blown
through Form, Line and Story
to form our human beings.

Murderers, the poet says, *are easily understood.*
But this: to hold
death, the whole of death, so gently
even before life's begun
and not go mad....

8.
Near dawn
someone stands over the canoe.
My mother over the bed.
She hands me a wood carving of a horse.
She tells me her father carved it
just before he died.

I lose the horse.
I drift in heartache, a flood of tears.
It is the only gift her father gave her,
the only gift she could give to me.

I find the horse again.
It is rough, but beautifully hewn.
I turn it in my hands
It is the heavy barrel of a gun.

A raven slips from the red water.
A band of horses reel off.
Mama, it is hard to find you
adrift the foundations
these hundreds of years

but how green are thy waters
how lofty the pines of thy breasts
how many little farms
nuzzle on your thighs

     9.   In The Night We Are Seen Waving Back To The Shore
We fall into her grief
from the valleys leading nowhere,
her pent-up aching rivers, her child
from the ruptured navel.

We rise to the constellation of Fish.
A horse on the beach slivered by the moon
presses its heavy face
to the water's skin.

From the waves the myth of us goes,
rises through her hooves,
whips through the long grass of the hill behind her.
She lifts her head.
In the black tunnels of empty, eternal space
that are her eyes
two blue flames
burn across the hemorrhaged lake.

Many animals come down to see us.
Their eyes are the fires of the first trappers
circling the beach.
They await our arrival,
the first people coming back.
But we push away

until the day breathes, the shadows flee away
and blue metallic dawn gathers in the low Appalache.
We cling to the ghost of a tree top

your arms like Neptune
your arms like musicians
from the halls of water
Now we come
to the sun

When I first knelt to you
before the fire in Albion
and witnessed in the flames' illumination
the swing of my breasts over you
and the deep eye from which my children have come
coming down onto you, beautiful
beautiful man
risen before the flames

I vowed I would come to this lake
to find your mother

Now the sun. *O pines, whisper of fish*
up through the shafts of light!
A woman's heart entombed in glass
O, refugee

we rise
to meet the sun.
Now who is it comes
up from wilderness?

Mother

An elegant black hearse
from the twenties
carries a baby coffin
in its sun-pierced, curtained windows
through the raw streets.

I listen to its weeping passage,
the ancient motor heaving across cobblestone,
each rotation of the old wheels
like first steps, like seeds

and the rusty sough of the wind,
an eagle sweeping close to the ground,
calling back years, my mother,
the people lost.

Dream image, July 4, 1976

     1.
There were four brothers
who went down to Southport
beneath Wilmington, North Carolina

They were fishermen, sailing
shrimpboats up to Boston

in search of a living
the longing in us
to get out
onto the high seas
to get out
of all the known
places

the faces on the high road
beyond the red curtains of my car where I sleep,
the ache, she always named it
Wanderlust, the sailor in your blood, she said
why the bobbing lights on the long poles
of the salmon boats at Mendocino
made me cry the first time I came around the beach
opening day of season

One was named Christopher Columbus Simmons,
her grandfather. Restless,
he sold his share in the boat,
went up the Cape Fear River,
took up farming.
But he had Wanderlust so bad
soon as he'd get his crop in
he'd take off again, the family in tow.

195

We were hungry.
So he went out to shoot a turkey or a deer.
But he couldn't find a turkey or a deer
so he shot a cow.
Then the sheriff was after him.
So we left in the night,
went down the river,
caught the train to Danville.

The Seminoles split off from the Creeks
disappeared south into the Florida Everglades.
As a matter of pride they named themselves
Samona,
Runaway

The Cherokee
who just slipped off
the Trail of Tears and all the dying
into the hills, where no one noticed

this unselfing the self
to cut new trails, a road to the left,
to hide out in the mountains, to just
go away

this family
seatossed here a hundred years before the Revolution,
always the ones who left,
these orphans who ache to be Indian, this forever
starting over, this mania, this outlawing, these westwalkers,
this running to be
unknown

There were 1300 Clarkes here
before the Revolution.
Some dropped the E. As a matter of pride
some retained it.

The one with Lewis
who crossed the continent in 1804

and Simmons, John, Christopher Columbus' father
who *was with Lee at Appomattox*
when he surrendered.
He walked home barefoot, 400 miles
smoking opium for his wounds.
The carpetbaggers wanted his plantation.
He was riding across Town Creek Swamp.
A bullet was fired, went through his vest,
hit Myrtle's crib inches above her head.
So we gave up the plantation.
He said it wasn't worth it.
We went to another place,
became tenant farmers.

But Suzannah Willits kept that vest in her trunk,
carried it wherever we went.
She had raised the sheep, then sheered,
washed, dyed, spun, cut and sewn it.
John sat in the corner and smoked opium
for his Civil War injuries.
They sent him into Wilmington
to take the cure.
He wasn't cured but they passed the law.
He'd go out of his mind.
He tried to kill Christopher Columbus with an ax.
He went down to the river, took off all his clothes.
He was going to jump in
but he said the water was too cold.

The Yankees burned Asheville's City Hall.
The records were lost
but so many of the women
in the other branches of the tree
have only one name, the same name:
Squaw: Cherokee, *Squaw:* Seminole, *Squaw:* Choctaw

The one who loved music at 16
and her German music teacher.
She had a child in 1885, *Olive*
and was ostracized by the town.
But Christopher Columbus loved her.
He said when he married her
before she grew fat with his ten children
he could circle the little globe of her waist with both hands
and his fingers would touch.

She loved flowers.
Regardless of how old or barren the house
we would move into
in Grandpa C.C.'s wanderings
Lizzie would make it beautiful
with flowers. I never see a hollyhock,
a snapdragon, a daisy
without seeing her.

And no one has ever known
or forgotten to wonder
what became of the child named *Olive*

or the other 16 year old, *Mary*
who boarded a train in 1900 at Wilmington
to meet the man she was to marry
in Asheville
and was never seen again.

The one walking along in France
during World War I
and he walked forward
and he looked back
and his head was falling off
and he was falling over

and he had nightmares of this
for the rest of his life

The redheaded Irish one
who walked the Dan River with his daughter
reciting the book of his hometown

Look Homeward Angel
to the children who worked in the mills,
to the one who shot a man in Jacksonville,
to Hester Andrews Clark, the first white person
to teach Blacks how to read after the Civil War
to the whole family dead in the Ivy Town Poor House
of the 1850 epidemic of small pox
to the rich uncle, R.J. Reynolds, who founded the tobacco company
to Libby Holme, the famous singer of the Twenties, he married, then murdered
to the cousins who still sit on the whittler's bench in Southport
to Aunt Belle who went home to the Reservation

to the cousin lost in World War II,
to the many Sundays of my childhood
we ate our picnic in the car
on the shady, treelined Southern California street
watching the door of her last known address
while Mama told the story again
of the sailor and her sister, Mozelle
I still call Aunt Ginny

His best friend married them.
But when he shipped out
she didn't hear from him.
The Red Cross informed her
he was married to someone else

to her mother dead at 25
to her father dead at 39

to the one who married Christopher Columbus and witnessed
seven of her ten children die
of tuberculosis

of the *thing* still carried
in the breath of my children.
Once a doctor asked me
if the family was from North Carolina
as if the place itself
tells the story
of swampy, humid lungs

to most of the family dead
of tuberculosis

    2.   Look Homeward Angel: Susie and Guy, The Wedding Picture
    a.
They will keep the vow, they will die very young.
It is World War I. She holds the American flag between them,
twirls the stick across her red-white-and-blue striped dress.
Beneath her bonnet of daisies and doves
she is tickled and she is already
waiting, Scottish lass with only a hint
of the Cherokee, Choctaw, and Seminole
so prominent in her last.
She tilts her head to him
as if she listens for something.

The thick red waves lift from his pale forehead.
The boymouth is suspicious, afraid
over the bow-tie, the high-buttoned tweed coat
the texture of tobacco. He's the mill child
before the child labor laws. A man married his mother
to put her children to work.
Guy was ten, he wanted to learn to read.
He ran away.

Her brother will come home from the war
with the Great Flu, the despair of 1918.
Everyone was afraid. Only she will nurse him.
My mother was playing in the yard
when she looked in the window
saw him die
of the disease of the breath
tuberculosis
that will consume the family, leave her
orphan.

Guy ran to the hills, to other women.
But Susie's breath is in him.
Though the stars of the states
are blowing through his hair in a wild red wind
and the stripes, for *purity* and *the blood*
fall between them, he'll not escape.
Runaway, that redheaded Irishman
my mother still looks for.

He married women she wouldn't call mother.
But I named my son for the Dan River where they walked,
the wild girl and the man whose hair was as red as the banks,
the river's rush from the hills still in her breath
and his *Look Homeward Angel* he recited by heart.

Something happened.
He killed a man in a poker game.
After a year in prison he escaped
with a key slipped to him in a potato.
She read the papers about *Guy Clarke*. He had friends.
Messages were whispered to her,
he's hiding in the hills of North Carolina.
She sat in the window, planned her escape.

When he was brought back for trial
he was found innocent. He'd shot in self-defense.
But he died in surgery to remove the breath
of this girl, Susie, my grandmother

who rose on the Easter morning of her death
to bake apples for him, their three babies.
They knew then she would get well.
My mother always told me flowers bloom
when they know they're dying.

     b.
Years later my old lover catches me in the street
of a far-western city.
I beg him to have mercy, to leave me alone.
He says he can't live unless I forgive him.

When I reach to touch him
I see how old my hands have grown.
I see that he still looks at me
with murder in his eyes.

I tell him I have moved
to the northwestern border of the country.
I live in a primitive cabin
that looks across the water to Canada.
I tell him of the beautiful poet
who also lives in the cabin.

But I leave often. I go out on the highway
and drive.
It doesn't matter that I have no money.
I pick-up hitchhikers for the gas.
I sleep in my car, dream
of having a baby with the poet
who never leaves
the cabin on the border.

I see in my old friend
two things I must tell him.
The first is that I dream of him.
These dreams come before the letters arrive
with the same news.
The second is that I may die
of sexual lonliness.
I still can't separate
my body from my mind, my heart from my psyche,
my poetry from the politic, the erotic from love.
The loneliness of these parts
well up in my body
in continuous, unbearable orgasm.
But even though I go out on the highway to sleep
I no longer look for him.

Remember, I say, touching his face
with the old flowers that are my hands,
how we used to speak of the soul's
yearning to be a body?

     3.   Garnet. Her Name Is Glass, Transparent Red

They buried her mother
wearing the watch
she had given to her.
She was four. All her life
she will wake in the night
to the ticking on her mother's hand
keeping time
under the ground.

What is it, Roethke asks, to be a woman?
To be contained, to be a vessel,
to prefer a window to a door,
a pool to a river?

My mother is a poem I'll never be able to write.
In my dreams I've committed a terrible crime.
I had no choice. Now I am running.
There was the particular ferocity
of the campaign to exterminate
the Seminoles with bloodhounds.
My mother is a poem I'll never find.
They want her to be the Reservation,
deep soil to the blowing seed, the settled one
who hates the road.

But as a girl in the orphanage
she watched the road out the window.
She always had to have a window to plot her escape.
She grew ill if the curtains were drawn,
if she didn't have a far view
to the road beyond the hills
to another century when she crosses the country
in a covered wagon.

She ran into the woods, lived on berries.
When they formed parties to search for her
she hid in a tall tree
until they quit calling
Garnet... Garnet...

Her name is of precious glass,
a deep transparent red.
But then she changed her name.
They say her father had red hair, they say
her mother, *Samona,* way back, they say two men
drove along the road at midnight looking for her.
But she ran through the woods,
got a safe ride, went to another town.

In the rearview mirror a girl
with a baby tied in a scarf to her back
lies down on the highway to sleep.
Shall I have another child?
I remember Helena Blavatsky
crossed the country twice in a covered wagon
for the experience of it

my mother, my orphan
country. She visited
her grandfather, Christopher Columbus, in jail.
He had bootlegged for a rich man
who went free. When he was released
he said he'd lost his heart
to live. He asked her for a chair.
When he sat down
he died.

I don't know why she is hard to find.
She has given me all the stories.
She is the story line of this poem. My mother, my
optimist

In the dream she hands me a horse
carved by her father just before he died.
It is newly rough-cut
without oil or varnish.
It is the only gift her father gave her.

I lose the horse.
I couldn't find her.
I couldn't find this poem.

When I find the horse again
it is a gun in my hands.
It is power, this poem
I am finally writing, the rough,
true art of these stories,
the gift I have.

The Cherokee, Choctaw and Seminole
buried their dead infants
as the boundary lines of their nations.
My mother settled into the nations of Mother
with the same unconditional allegiance.

She had three babies in three years.
Flowers became her escape.
I looked out the window once
saw her lie down in their bed.

My mother is a poem I'll never write.
In her as John Muir says
one may think the clouds themselves
are plants.

4.   *O Wild Girl Wilderness, Thrown Seed*
They were going to put me in a reform school.
I was 15 and unhappy. I would just walk away.
There was this man I never did like, old man Towell.
He was a former Danville policeman and everyone loved him,
hugged him and things, but I'd stay back.
I just wasn't the type. He did little diggy things.
Once he told a large crowd
of taking a welfare package to my home at Christmas.
I was so embarrassed. I hated him.
At first he was just superintendent of the farm,
but when I got older he was made Assistant Superintendent
of the whole school.
I'd run away and he'd come after me.
He'd threaten to take my pants down and whip me. Imagine,
I was 15. I hated that man.
I'd pick up a stick and dare him to do it.

I ran away to find my father.
I was 15. He was 27 miles away.
He'd gotten out of the sanitarium
and was helping some people on a farm,
the only kind of work he could do.
I left in the night, hitched,
got picked up by two men
who made advances.
I got out on this lonely road and hid.
They drove the car back and forth looking for me.
I went up to a farmhouse. It was 2 am.
I knocked on the door. A man's voice said
"Go down to the next farm. They take in strays."
I went down to the next farm. A man's voice asked
"Who is it?" I said, "It's me." The man said
"Answer the door, dear. There's a little nigger girl at the door."
So they gave me a daybed and I slept all night.
I woke to the smell of ham and eggs cooking. Oh,
it smelled so good and I was so hungry.
But when they asked me for breakfast I said,
"Oh, no thank you. I must be on my way."

I was so lonely walking away from there.
The smells of pancakes, ham and eggs
were coming from all the houses.
It was early Sunday morning and people
were coming out on the porches
to pick up their Sunday papers.
But then I walked through the woods and birds were singing
and the world was beautiful.
I met a colored woman washing her clothes in the creek.
I got within a mile of the place, Whittle's Depot
when old man Towell drove up.
"Get in," he said.
There was nothing I could do but get in.

5.   They Met In A Library

They met in a library in Charlotte, North Carolina.
His hand came from across the table,
pointed to the word
she sought but could not find.
Everyday she worked the crossword
before going to work
at the lunch counter on the corner.
He was unemployed, came in for the want ads.
She had the paper.

Together they finished the puzzle.
He walked her to work. She was an orphan
but never used that word. He was a black
sheep, he said, see how the people sneer
because I'm not wearing a tie.

Her grandfather was Christopher Columbus Simmons.
His grandfather was George Washington Chitwood.
They were married in three months, a union
from the want ads, the right word to the puzzle.
They went out west to that clean
city of angels
where no one sneered
at a man without a tie, a woman without ties.
They had three children.
The first was me, Rose of Sharon
from *The Grapes of Wrath,*
now a poet
in search of the word.

When Mama told me
about sex
she warned

I don't know what
your father and I would have done
if we couldn't have married
soon as we did. I'm afraid
we would have broken
those rules too.
I don't think
we could have helped it.

6. Coming Back From Myrtle Beach Sunburned In the Rumble Seat With
    Daddy Before They Are Married

They worked the tobacco fields in Stokesdale.
On Saturdays, half-day off, they went swimming,
or up to Winston-Salem to the shows.
They lived in Chattanooga all winter of '39.
He sold insurance in the Negro Debit.
Friday nights he worked until midnight to get the money
before they spent it all, knifed each other.

There were so many knifings
they didn't even record
Negro murders in Chattanooga

When they couldn't get work
they went home to Ducktown,
lived with his parents.
But the strikes were on in the mines.
After 40 years they couldn't make the rent.
Uncle K.D. came from California
to talk sense into Grandpa
against the union. When he saw it was no use
he urged his baby brother to go west with him.
But *under no circumstances* could a woman go.
They'd send for her later.

But she knew she'd never get to California
if he went without her.
They were all going to have to go up to Marion and Elizabeth's,
the only ones with a job. Uncle Marion worked for Tusculum,
the college. She wasn't going there.
Mill child, poor thing, uneducated, white trash, orphan, she was *not.*
If she wasn't going to California he wasn't going.
They had to take her.

When they were starting out
Grandma slipped her a secret quarter *just in case.*
She was 19, the only woman
of five men in the old Ford.
She would doze-off
fall on a shoulder not my father's.
They chewed bubble gum all the way
to plug the holes in the radiator,
to quiet the hunger pains.
They ate their only meal in Arizona.
They walked out without paying. Ran.
She thought they'd never make it across the desert
the way the Ford heated up.

But at the Colorado River she looked across to California
to *the Promised Land, the land of Milk and Honey.*
And at Cajon Pass
when she smelled the orange blossoms
she knew she had done the right thing
because the song kept coming to her
your purple mountains' majesty.

They survived in the beginning
by night raids on cornfields
in Torrance and Long Beach.
She and Aunt Alice wore the men's overalls
to stuff the golden-haired ears.
Daddy and Uncle K.D. drove along the outside
of the tall rows in the get-away car.
Mama always laughed when she told me
of the farmer on Rosecrans
who shot at her.

7.   Genesis: The First Story Ever Told Me

I was crying. I couldn't stop crying. I had been crying for three days. I wanted to see my mother. It was Easter. We knew she was very sick. I had almost died myself just 4 months before with double pneumonia so I knew what it was to be sick. It's my only memory of my father before her death. He sat by me all night, or many nights. Mama left us with her mother when she found out she had t.b. She went to stay with Daddy's mother. There were no sanitariums available. She was so afraid she would give us t.b. When she found out in October or November I was 3½, Lawrence was 6, Mozelle was only a little over a year.

We were in Reidsville, North Carolina, just over the Virginia line. Mama was outside Dansville, about 25 miles away. But we didn't have a car, so we didn't see her until Easter. Then we went to see her. Maybelle and her husband Odie took us. Easter was on the 20th of April that year, 1924. It was a deliriously happy day! Mama got up and cooked breakfast for us all. We had scrambled eggs and baked apples. I thought that apple was the most delicious food I had ever eaten. After eating mine, I wanted another one. Mama insisted on giving me hers. I was happy to get it but someone shamed me for taking it.

We were happy because we knew Mama was getting well, because her cheeks were flushed and she looked so pretty. Later we spent the night in Danville with her sister, Maybelle. That night we had jello, the first jello I had ever eatern. When we got up the next morning we had cornflakes, another new food. I loved them. After breakfast Maybelle told us that Mama had died in the night. Lawrence and I cried so hard and long that Maybelle told us that maybe it wasn't so, that she believed she was just sleeping. We would go to see her. She took us back to Grandma Hammet's house. Lawrence went in first to see Mama and came out crying. When I went in and saw her I could not cry. I remembered Maybelle saying she may be asleep. I had to believe that. Everyone in the house was crying. I tried to cry but I couldn't. Later at the funeral I put spit in my eyes to look like I was crying. I was terrified when they lowered her into the ground. All I could think was what will she do if she wakes up. She won't be able to get out. All my life I have had nightmares about this. I guess this is the cause of my claustrophobia.

I didn't cry when my Dad died either. Although I was 16—well, it was January, 1936, so I was only 15—I refused to see him after he died. I would not go to the funeral home and though Aunt Dora tricked me into going to the burial, I refused to get out of the car and would not look when they lowered him into the grave. I sat looking straight ahead and could hear them singing "Abide with Me" with one ear, and with the other "The Music Goes Round and Round" sung by someone off in the distance. This is one of the things Dora never forgave me and did not like me for. But I had had so many nightmares that he would die too that when it happened I told myself it was a dream. I would wake up. If I did not see it, it would not be so.

8.   I Want To Keep Putting A Road Into This Poem

I study her photograph
taken at the Pike in Long Beach
the month I am conceived.

She works a seashore stand
on the pier at Hermosa.
He drives the Good Humor Ice Cream truck
down Hollywood Boulevard, through Beverly Hills.
All over the world war rages.

From her beautiful face to anywhere
the road must go now
through rivers, mountains, oceans and time.
And through my mind, the faces
of my ancestors she has given me, fishermen
sailing up to Boston
in search of a living

from here to anywhere, out of the emptiness
the loops and holes that are not covered
in all the forces that bear down,
through these we come, the perfect child
unraveling in the present, the music
going round and round.

She sat by the window to nurse me.
The domestic task was so foreign
it was blood I first drank.
She was afraid of the breath
that had made her an orphan.
Her face looking down on me
was masked.

She heard on the wind her mother calling
through the orphanage walls.
She poured over the maps on the kitchen table
like a lover. She walked ahead in the road,
looked back, saw herself falling over.
She always said she'd never make it.
She died four times of the disease of the breath.
I always thought she was looking for her parents.
When she came back from the dream
she was leading them out.

But she hid in the tops of the trees when they called her name.
Her eyes are blue flames in the green mask of the leaves,
o, wild girl of the river I named my son for. *Mother,
Father. Brother. Sister. Daughter. Country.*
She summons them out of the flowers and stones,
on the road disappearing around the hill,
down the tracks of the one who was lost.
She hunts them to where the sea begins.
She rides a runaway horse through this poem,
a strange opium through my blood.
She tells me the stories, a search
for the living, a hidden road
out from
all the known places.

This is a poem that cannot end

*She comes to a gypsy camp in the woods.
A terrible crime has just occurred.
Dancing bears are tied to a tree
near the one she hides behind.
Men and bareshouldered women circle a fire,
play violin, accordion.*

*Then a wild-eyed, frightened man
runs past her.
He is chased by the police.
She doesn't know what he has done.
She doesn't care.
It is wrong that so many
chase one, evil
when they catch him.*

*They leave him handcuffed to a tree.
He is sobbing.
She slumps behind her tree, sobbing.*

*Then she goes down the road in search of an ax.
She will chop down the tree.*

Appalachian Song

I see a dirt road inside myself and on it I am walking.
At the far end where the sun is setting
are my children, all the western scattering
of my flesh.

Here are the voices I hear, the unaccountable melancholy,
the dark hearts of my grandparents, storied in my flesh.
When I look to the hills I hear
shattering like glass, the red in the loam
soaked from me.

Near the cabin at the clearing's center
I hear a mournful Scottish melody.
When I walk amidst flowering dogwood
a thousand tongues lift their words to me.

Call my name in the act of love. I am full of loss
and the shadowy Cherokee. At night I fall
into our migrations, settlers drifting across
the Great Barrier.

The cold winters you say, the loss of war paint,
the images tattooed on the skin of my brain.
My daughter in the river we drink, its body
lifting her before she knew the body of a man.

When you call me, your face, bald as the eroded hills,
is blessedly here, between me and these scenes.
But when we ride the boy in your scrotum, which stores,
like glass, the ruins of this place, you pull
houses full of blood, mountains full of smoke, down
on top of me.

Louisana

1.

We rise up over St. Tammany's Parish, swampforest,
white shore. Black figures stand
in the blue water gulf coast, out front
the Confederate President's last home.

We sleep inside the car, skin stuck to metal.
We try not to touch, afraid of the ground
moccasins, copperheads, two men
broken down.

He sleeps. From the wide door, by moonlight,
an oak in the bare expanse of savannah. Swampqueen
draped in white mossy dress, Evangeline, dragging behind
her cloudflowing robes, her moonwhite hair.

Her moanwhite sighs. I dream the famous phantom head
of the blond actress queen
soaring low like a silver bird along the bayou.
I dream I am living in a primitive village.
A Cajun Queen works on my teeth.
Her long robes and white hair drape my face.
On the dusty road home where flocks of snow white pelicans wade
I find his diary written months before
he brought this lover to me.
I hide in the withered sedge
to read his secret thoughts.
I give birth to a child in the swamps,
conceived while I flutter in the form of a hawk
over his dead form.

I wake to a moaning diesel napping off the asphalt sleep,
to the bayou suffocating in thick white hair.
I wake to you, angry, the last time
we make love, listening,
as you soar, a great bird, above me
to the Singing River of the Pascagoula
the legendary chant of tribesmen, who, facing defeat,
are marching into the river.

2.   Bayou, Choctaw *Bayuk, Small Stream*
The southern end where all her water is flushed.
Causeways are humped monsters, miles of cement feet
stuck in swampwater, backwater, motor boats
zip around trees standing dead white
in the flushed sewage.

Sticky Biloxi. Black Baptists
circle white steeple, pastels,
darksuited splotches stand around
on the Sunday pineprairie

Swamprabbit, now sugar in these cane lands
Dark sweaty
secrets

the Mississippi boy he was in jail with,
fantastic storyteller, nothing else to do
all winter, cooped in your swampshack,
tell stories, kill your girl.

     3.   Beau Bridge off Causeway
Redoak jointsnake camass, Bayou Teche,
painted words on cement bridge. *Boudin*
is blood sausage, blood sausage of Molly Bloom,
this is the way to go down, southdown, Beau Bridge, real place
to eat *Catahoula white*
crawfish.
Arcadians, French from Nova Scotia,
Creeks, also refugees, welcomed them.
Called Cajuns, Evangeline,
the story of their sorrow. Cajun Queen
Buttle la Rose sargassumfish

Leaving. The sky opens: the West
a vast abstraction
BayouCourtableauAudubonShearwater

The Northwest is open.
The Southwest is piled up.
Lightning divides them

watertupelo home

Little white houses on stilts
walk the savannah.
BayouCourtableauAudubonShearwater
Mary and Jesus, French, huddled
in small roadside rockhuts.

     4.   Lake Charles
Drinking Pearl, he drives me around
the old neighborhood, the boarding house
he lived in ten years ago, eight dollars
a month, the older woman who took him in,
the extra oomph to get you over
being so far from home, the Texas State Line,
the mossplain, Sabine River, raining hard,
riding hard the green mirror
as far as you can see:

tremulous broken silver sky

Passing us 80 miles per hour, muscular
short-haired black worker
against East Texas oilfields
downing something in a thermos

as he heads for doubletime, Sunday,
moonlight. As he heads home to Houston,
from weekend with the kids, coffee, whiskey, soup,
anything: To *keep going.*

     5.   Drinking Lone Star   Bought at Bergeron
Truckstop, guy yells across room
when I walk in
Hey Waitress!

Then the boss coos
Would you like a job?
looking at me through
the black lines she's drawn
to find her eyes, her sixty blond years.
Redneck in me
still shows.

The world is turning pink and grey
leaving through the screen door
and I am here in Texas.
He continues *the East, the dark area*
where doubting Thomas went.

What is local is rhythm
the rhythm systems of the United States,
the path the wind takes to shape the body,
the path the body takes to find the heart.

Cow in bayou, birds follow
in its footsteps, crossing
the Trinity River, sweet Jesus, the toke,
rising into

sunset flash, mirrored in a thousand flooded lakes,
emerald, *fata morgana, lady in the lake,*
pelicans

Lost and Old Rivers

Old whitehaired black woman
hunched, walking back
the gulfcoast causeway

6.   Houston

I was a nocturnal person heavy into the dope scene.
Friends shooting up acid, I thought police
were watching my house.

Horse galloping alongside, kicking dust,
147 miles to San Antonio, the way intimacy
is lost the more you know someone.
Toledo Bend, Caddo, Texoma, as if
to protect your own story, no other state
so many rodeos, or secret
Polish colonies in exile.

7.   The Temperaments

A fifty year old man was left hanging on a road sign
last week by two hitchhikers who pistol whipped him.
A miracle he survived, the paper says.

A preacher didn't stop
for the man hanging on the road sign.
I'd probably do the same thing again.
There have been several murders around that area.
I have to think of my family.

When the victim was asked
he said he'll probably continue
to pick up hitchhikers.

Probably. I've always done it.
I believe in helping people.

Travels With Charlie: How Far Does The World Extend?

1.
Oaks turn to tall sage.
The Apaches, standing together, dim Mexico.
Windmills thirst, crank and fuss the wide open spaces,
wide forever, *who for her hunger shall I say*

He says there's room here for all New England,
all the middle Atlantic states and Illinois, and still
space left over. We're so far south the Scorpion
crawls the horizon on its belly.
We come to the Staked Plains. The Padres marked the trail
by staked buffalo skulls.

When I think of this country, he says,
I think of an axis between New York and Los Angeles.
Texas is the spiral, inside of which is empty,
just a guy in a tower shooting at everyone.

Days it takes you to cross. Now the earth is red.
Rain catches the great play of colors, sucks
flesh-colored bark, pinyons, Texas Ladylegs.
Suzanne takes you down the altered sky, the grey ocean
expanse, swell upon swell, billowing tent top, blooming
cacti, *thank god*, Thoreau said, *they can't cut down
the clouds.*

2.
He says, his silhouette against the Apaches,
If I was rich, I'd be an alcoholic. It feels good.

We roll down the road, the driver drunk, the asphalt
rolls up in us, miles of white line, space and rain.
He asks me why I'm crying, then says he's just like Steinbeck.
*A pisces too. His wife said he was difficult
to live with also.*

I look down at my hands in the window
to the mirror of moving sage, red soil,
where we've been, my flesh too old
beneath mountains, in whose lacy form
a funnel of rain is poured.

He pulls over. He stands there murmuring
Desert and thunder whisper *yess*
over the snakey-hiss of his piss. Now
a ghost rises from the highway sage he hits.
Poncho Villa to the clouds. Now
the darkblue violet swallows us. *Texas*, he says
has karmic connections with Tennessee.

3.

What I'm saying, One Country. Four main drifts.
East to West, the Great Push. Before that
crossing Appalachia, Southwest, part of which
ends up ultimately
in Texas

Crime, family, a woman on your trail, shady
circumstances, you'd say
GTT, hang a sign on your door
GTT

Gone To Texas

4.

The pioneers saw prairie fires on the horizon,
the whole western sky
black at sunset

Days they advanced on the source
Days of speculation, preparation, dread

but it was only
a million bats
spiraling at dusk
out of the caverns

5.

What made these shapes, this geography?
Who, for her hunger, shall I say

Evangeline wandered her whole life across these sands
in search of her stolen country

What made this geology?

The ocean at Mendocino tearing into the bluffs,
ships and sailors sucked unaccountable miles
east beneath the land

What made this place, this history?

The slave woman who escaped Coronado's expedition
in Palo Colorado
who then wandered east
free across the waste
until she was caught
by De Soto's expedition
on the Trinity River

What made this weather?

The bones found this week in the wreckage
of a World War II bomber
the remains of at least three, perhaps five

What made this soul?
The Bibles that the pioneers bound
in Indian skin.

What made this land, this heartache?
The Earth yearning, pulling the human back

the astronauts, who when trouble occurred
begged

Bring us back
to burn up in the earth's atmosphere.
Don't let us fall
down the icelocked cone of space.

6.

On the radio a woman in Alabama
sends out the call every ten minutes.
Diesel with red stripes left Oregon yesterday.
Call home immediately. Please. Call home now.

Windmills pull from flat sage
the Ogaleilla underground, its million year old
water

Train tracks, telephone poles carry
in a straight line your voice
stretching across worlds, tracks across
years the empty land

Help me to find him.
Somewhere he's out there.

Sheffield: oil
and the poor tumble in desert wash, javalinas
snort and wallow

an old man eats lunch in the Cactus Cafe

down in the thicket, a black bull
rests his heavy head
on the rump of his cow

a dressed-up young woman
descends the only thing for miles,
the stairs of her mobile home,
now makes her highheeled way
through sage

travelers, you descend
these dry-burnt buttes, down
across the Pecos
and out

sun, wind, in the distance
you remember
Russia, Mandelstam's last poem
through Kiev, through the streets of the monster
a wife is trying to find her husband.

Austin: The Making of a Boy

1.

In the museum they blame his mother.
Rebecca Baines.
But he always defended her,
"the great lady," "the perfect woman,"
"brilliant," "sexy," "beautiful,"
"endlessly enchanting."

She felt very much alone
in the jackrabbit country of the Pedernales
on the north bank, in Stonewall,
Blanco County
where he was born.

My mother soon learned my daddy was not a man
to discuss higher things. His idea of pleasure
was to sit up half the night drinking beer
with the fellows, telling stories, playing dominoes.
The first year of her marriage
was the worst year of her life.

Then I came along
and everything
was all right again.

The burden, he says, *you have no idea,*
begging his cabinet, *and anyone*
to come up with the answer.

At three I could recite
long passages of Longfellow,
Tennyson. The minute I finished
she'd take me in her arms,
hug me so hard I sometimes thought
I'd be strangled to death.

On my first hunting trip
with my daddy
I vomited
on the rabbit.

Was I coward
or what
he wanted
to know

After that
I refused
violin lessons,
her instructions
in elocution.

The burden, you have no idea.
The men of ideas think little of me
but I chose
to talk like him.
A man.

2.
One day, the year before he died,
he took his biographer, a Harvard graduate,
on a long car ride.
He wanted to confess
that all along
he'd been hiding the fact
that she reminded him of his dead mother.

In talking to you
I have come to imagine
I am talking to her

Before I die
I need to master
some understanding
of what happened in my life,
and of who I am

3.
Visitors to the ranch were handed rifles,
expected to shoot an antelope or a deer.
Politicians and bureaucrats
were called upon to swim naked
with him in the White House pool.
Members of the cabinet and White House staff
were compelled
to accompany their boss
into the bathroom
to continue their conversation.

4.
In the museum the largest displays
are his daughters' wedding dresses.
The dress of the daughter who hated him
is ruffles, romantic gossamer.
The dress of the one who honored him
is of classic lines.

5.
In the movie he walks arm in arm
with his wife whose name is bird.
His heart is bad.

The burden, you have no idea.
I don't know
any more
what's right

He points to the giant oak
he climbed
at the ceremony for his grandfather.
When the coffin was lowered into the ground
he felt something within him
bang shut

you have no idea

walking away, shoulders collapsed,
his long hair falling down his back,
her hand, whose name is Lady, plunged
all the way through
his curls

     6.   Dallas, *The Linga Sharira*
I dream I am in the car
when the President is assasinated
by a man in a light grey suit
who has always been with me.
My understanding is even greater
than my horror and grief.
I leave the car through the window, awkwardly,
a smaller, less glamorous version of his wife,
like a swimmer in danger of drowning,
to tell the world what has happened

but I find I am emerging to a shore
of faceless men in dark grey suits.

El Paso del Norte

I travel the carved cities that straddle the Rio Grande,
the bottom of the Rockies, looking for Desdemona,
named by her Juarez mother for the wife Othello killed,
the girl in the Pacific surf made naked by a wave.
When he touched her breast, Angel, a marine from El Paso,
asked her to marry him.

Street angel. His shelter was a garbage can
in an alley in Juarez. Little Tigua,
the oldest identifiable people.
He would never forget the hunger.
Consuelo Maria Gonzales watched him from her high windows
that winter he thought he was eight.
She left him food on the bridge
in crannies the others couldn't find.
She named him Angel because he had the most beautiful face
she had ever seen. She took him as her son, for time,
as security against her old age.

Which came, a moldy aristocracy
that went on for years everlasting
for Desdemona in a tract Four-Bedroom
in the dying orange groves east of Pomona.
Together we sowed grass seed to the talus lawns,
raked boulders under smoggy sun and hot winds
that slammed down the 5000 foot San Gabriel wall,
sucked off the desert by a vacuum.

Inside, the drapes drawn, the house boiled
in sour chilies, prickly pears.
Consuelo Maria Gonzales held court
in the foreign country of her cracked mind
and thin skin. Desdemona fed and bathed her
as each child came, as Angel trucked the L.A. basin,
a van and storage man, his time to care for her now.
But it was the wife who slaved over her, who prayed
her dead, who yearned for sex without dread of her cruel abuse.
The witch, she cursed, is 96, and still not dead.

Consuelo Maria finally died on a Sunday ride.
As always, Angel carried her out to the drive,
folded her long body of sticks
into the backseat of the Volkswagon.
She died at the intersection of Ramona and Indian Hill Boulevard.
She stiffened instantly and her bowels moved.
Desdemona, driving, secretly rejoiced.

Angel lost his mind.
With his mother dead he was free to truck
crosscountry for the money. But the driving, the nights
without sleep, the nights without food or anyone to talk to,
crossing back and forth on speed, moving mattresses
and photographs from old home to new house,
suspect even at the truckstops, the Indian behind the wheel,

this oldest identifiable person, the most beautiful
face ever seen on the cold concrete trails
over the lit houses of America
where human beauty is feared most of all,
lost his mind, forgetting, Desdemona cried,
not just to communicate, but what to say altogether.

The sun set behind the eucalyptus windbreak to the orange grove,
a thousand dying suns, the three-block stucco track buried deep within.
Every evening the crows returned to the trees
from some secret place in the basin still fertile,
circled and screamed from tree to tree, blackening
the sky that rendered gold, dusty rose. I saw Angel
deep inside the garage mouth, the cold black space
the head of a crow, the garbage can he once starved in.
He stared out at me, pissed, hungry, exposed, his hand
the flapping wing of an oldest avenging angel.
Around his savage head hung the pink bodies of young girls
marking time, the garage where the father forever bends
to his saw, to the mind lost from the mother.

She stiffened instantly and could not be unbent.
She should have died years ago, Desdemona wept,
she was such a bitch she could put off Death.
Now its possession was immediate and contagious
to the mind of her husband. The car filled
with the horrendous mud of her body. *Swamprot,*
she sobbed. For years I've smelled it.

They drove.
They went out the San Bernardino Freeway,
then back down Baseline, Angel crying.
They went home. They struggled to free her from the car.
She wouldn't unbend. As she had done for years,
Desdemona bathed her mother-in-law.
Again, they drove.
In Ontario they pulled into a mortuary.
Angel returned to the car, his face
for the first time the face when he lost his mind.
They drove away through the foothills in that strangest
of all countries, the San Gabriels, Angel crying
he remembered something. Something he almost forgot.

They dug through the rocky ground, granite
fallen five thousand feet, racing the sun
to work her from the backseat without breaking her. Somewhere
north of the Cucamonga Winery, in the talus beneath Mt. Baldy
they buried his mother, Consuelo Maria Gonzales,
in the sitting position she died in,
the way they buried the dead, as Angel remembered,
in the old world, rather than force her
to unbend.

Petrified Forest

The gates of the forest are locked.
The wind howls through the stone trees,
reams the painted desert
where young Navajo mothers
fill their wide skirts with paper and debris
then set themselves on fire.

In the parking lot the wind blows
the expensive clothes and hair
of a beautiful woman
who is climbing into a sports car
next to her twin husband.
Every gesture reveals
she thinks she is the star
of a movie located elsewhere.

But something beyond that is strange. Human.
Something startles me.
Her face begins to pull mine
as if I know her, an old friend,
the girl I have loved the longest.

And then everything, *Love!*
within a wind that eats stonebark,
is reaching out from me towards her,
and within me, against the wind
that wants to level everything,
rock remembers tree, psyche's ache
to liberate her sister.

Still, I hold myself from running to her, *Listen...*
Remember? Don't you remember?
and lean, a crumbling ruin in a whirl of sand,
against the cool stucco of the visitor's center.
A few of the ones who believe stonetrees
are the spirits of their dead
pass in silence. Her eyes
pass over all of us, remembering nothing.

Then they roar away, heading west.
The winds, our million mouths,
scream the ache after her.

Arizona
Every year the Kachinas come to help the people, bringing blessings
from other stars, worlds, and people.

1. Ramona

Ramona is laughing at herself
lying in a pool of her aborted child's blood.
The dark bawl of a cow's grief for its calf
taken by men today for veal
pulls north her adobe's beefblood floor.
The cow won't leave the place she last saw it
and she won't quit her bawl for three days. *Her crying,*
Ramona says, *will keep the children awake. She's why*
I quit meat. The herd, though unfenced,
hovers the adobe as if in dread of open range,
the foreign country just feet away
and the ancient oaks grown up as dwarves.

The valley is named Miracle.
The word is the valley's only neon:
a cold blue light over this 5000 foot border night.
Miracle, where the heat, she says, of Coronado's march
into what has become this country
was recently photographed.

Her husband is gone.
He left her bleeding their fourth child into the bed
to join a search party in Mexico
for five missing white men. Her face is landlocked,
pale and twisted as the moon's light on dwarfed oaks.
I think a part of the child is still in me.

We are old friends, Ramona and I, we laugh,
listen for stories, her dead brother to come back.

He put a plastic bag over his head. In Tucson, November 22.
The night before, she was pulled from sleep to the window.
Beyond the pillow and crumpled blanket
she saw her neighbor in the moonlight,
local lore has as member of the Family
the killers of the last decade,
cloaked in a black cape
rise up out of the border wash
and call across the desert for followers.

The night before her brother took his life I dreamed
I walked the end of the land in Mendocino.
The ocean thundered from the west, from the south, from the north
at a dark tangle of people trapped between the sea
and the old corrals at Cuffey's Cove
where the telephone cable comes in from the Orient.
The corral kept them on the narrow ledge of the continent,
kept them from coming ashore.
From the dark their voices whined at me.
Their arms stretched to me through the fenced spaces.
They ran its length as I walked on the free side,
a fast clamor of terrified bodies, *Please, please*
they called after me, like the grieving cow now. *Please.*

But when I looked to answer
I couldn't see who they were or what they wanted.

And then I was awakened to write these clear, blue words:
But merely to SEE
                (it is easy)
beyond the blue of the flesh
and the round pulling of the story
is oaktrees, is easy, is
oaktrees

2.   *The Earth With Her Bars Around Us Forever*
The State prepares Eminent Domain to take her land
for Coronado's Memorial. The neighbors
truck organic vegetables from the part of the valley
that is Mexico to Los Angeles, though local lore
says they are really in the dope business
and any day you can walk the mile to the bordergate
and see the truck sprayed. Today she took me
to the Bisbee Saloon to see if any of the miners
in the old photograph is my grandfather, but the faces
were like constellations whose lines I can't quite draw,
like the faces the Indians here see in stones they dig from the ground.
The Lavender Pit closed this year, after ninety-five
and the town debates its future: ghost town, artist retreat,
or tourist trap, *like Tombstone,* she says, *the idea of the place*
more authentic than the place ever was.
But Cananea, across the border, still shoots its copper shit
into Miracle Valley. *Borders can't stop some things,* she continues
as we sit in this room high over the midnight land
that also floats the blue *Miracle, like the immanent spirits*
that float on the domain of air, though it is strange,
recalling the bull that chased her, overdue, into Mexico,
my children will live in a different world than those born there.
We are old friends, laugh how Cananea is where Nino Cochise,
104, and living down the road, worked his first white man's job
shooting union strikers in 1915, while miners from Bisbee
were hauled out to the desert to die, as today
on the table between us, two wetbacks, pistol-whipped,
and castrated by a local rancher
were left to die in the desert.

And Nino, grandson of Cochise, nephew of Geronimo
escaped at fifteen into Mexico
with his mother and a small band
of old men, women and children
and reestablished, despite starvation, depression, disease,
in a hidden desert canyon in Sonora,
while the men waged guerrilla war,
the Apache Way.

In the tradition, transmitted by his mother
and a century-old medicine man
while the American and Mexican governments
hunted them and Geronimo reigned terror for them
he undertook the grueling
physical and spiritual training
of an Apache Chief, fasted weeks
on a two foot wide sandstone shelf
hundreds of feet over the canyon,
spent months preparing for marriage
so crucial was the work of husband,
became a warrior, a killer, in defense of the Way,
a lover and devoted husband,
fierce spiritual guide for his people
starting over.

They survived.
Eighteen years passed.
The boys grew to be men.
The U.S. and Mexican posses
no longer searched for them.
His wife died. The World
became the Twentieth Century.
Nino Cochise, 36, restless, bored,
at the bottom of a lost canyon
heard it calling to him.
He resigned as Chief, left his people
wandered out of the canyon
into the rest of the world.

He went to Hollywood,
became an Indian in the movies

and I, lost in Ramona High,
hungry for the Twentieth Century,
twirled the baton and led the girls
down roads and highways
behind Nino, Grand Marshall
of the Ramona Turkey Day Parades,
highstepped in my sequins, my flung
and flaming bar,
over the shit
of his horse

3.   Eminent Domain

For days now state vehicles have been appearing
on the dirt road outside, the hard lines
of the drivers' faces, like those in the dream
on the edge of the country,
the old photograph
contracted beyond human recognition
to the United States,
as if these miles of unguarded border
threatened even their gringo good looks

as was understood of the white Christians
who sang in their churches
after the treaty of Guadelupe Hidalgo
which ended the war

Green Grow The Rushes Oh!
the words floating, like imminent spirits
on the domain of air, both sides
the new border, the etymology
of *Gringo*

The radio is telling of UFOs
spotted directly over this part of the border
1 a.m. this morning. *They come from all over,*
Ramona laughs, *for the miracles.*

4.

Before Arizona was a state
my grandfather was a miner here.
One evening as the sun went down
on his desert shack, a dying Navajo boy appeared.
My grandfather, who had wanted to be a doctor
but was unable to for money
lifted the boy from his horse
and carried him to his bed.

When the boy was healed of syphilis and gone
and the sun was setting again
Grandpa looked up to find himself
surrounded by mounted Navajos
bearing gifts for the man
who had saved the life of a chief's son.

The chief's robe hung above Grandpa's bed
when he was dying of miner's lung.
He called me to his side.
Goldilocks, come here, Goldilocks.
Even when his huge paw hands
held mine, he still called
Goldilocks, come here

as did my uncle who was dying,
who held my hand and told the story
into my recorder
of my grandfather in Arizona,
who with his crippled leg
and ache to stay in the west,
his panic to get out of the Tennessee mines,
his love of the body,
his desire to be a doctor,
became instead
the hangman
in Globe, Arizona.

5.   Sky Pilot
we put miniature airplanes
all over his casket
all different kinds ·
all over his flowers

one biplane silhouetted
atop the great mass
of white chrysanthemums

Before they closed it
my brothers put them all
but one
in the casket with him
and in his coat pocket
a solo flight plan

6.
Old highway 66
the road with your brother
into the foothills
before he lost his mind
past Cucamonga wineries
Old Baldy stone houses
of early homesteaders, crumbling

like our fifteen year old neighbor from his motorcycle
whose death we are grieving
The dark clouds of the San Gabriels, your brother is saying
are hovering like the veils of an old widow

And coming years later by greyhound down Oregon mountains
through Roseville, I looked west
beyond the blue walls of the place
he was crazy in, the VA Hospital
to see the clamor of bodies
behind the dark fence
pleading for me as I went

7. Ramona,
I kissed goodbye the howling beast on the borderline which separated you from me.

Now we walk the midnight border.
Miracle Valley circles like mounted Navajo.
Like a waterline, you say, *this used to be a lake.*
I find shells, rocks that used to be
fish. You can dance the border. You climb the fence
reach back for me.

The animals and gods of the sky
come down to the shore to drink
the way the frame of the world sloshed through me
when I read your letter of his death.
You point north to the distant ranch lights
of the fifteen year old boy who came through your window.
You refuse to call it rape.
You lift your leg high over our country,
swing it south over the foreign country,
then dance me west over two graves, stone words
clear in the moonlight of the intent to go back
to both countries. You jump down into Mexico,
take aborted blood from your body, gather grave dirt.
The child will come back from both countries.
Then you meet my eyes, *I hardly care about him,*
my husband, the outside. This border
is why I stay.

8. *Ramona*
There are real borders.
The Hopi have sealed the outer boundaries of this land
with the blood of a young boy and girl
sacrificed in grief and prayer
at the source of the Colorado River.
Some of their blood was poured into the river
to circle the western boundary
and some of it was carried in a sacred jar
and poured into the source of the Rio Grande
to circle the eastern boundary.
The state cannot take their land.
No man can rape me.

9. Ramona, *The Linga Sharira*
We stand together, facing south, looking down the cone,
the long body of the past, the spiral nebulae
extending through the Galaxy's time,
the ecliptical world, lit by whirling planets,
to the center and source of the Milky Way,
Sagittarius, the beginning of the White Rainbow.

In you, Ramona, I learned the stars.
In your brother I have learned how
every year on the day he killed himself,
the day between Scorpio and Sagittarius,
our Solar System, a pin-point vessel
that rises as though on a wave
cutting across the galactic sea,
sails into a perfect right angle
to the Long Body of the Milky Way
and receives on that day, on that day only,
the direct full rays of the Universe's source and center,
the creative explosion from which we are propelled.

The ancients who lived out under the stars
knew the structure of our Galaxy.
They knew the Procession of the Poles
created time traps for hapless souls
due to the ecliptical and equatorial crossroads of the equinoxes.
They knew this eternal route,
the Crossroads of Time and the Universe,
our Galaxy's crossroads with the ecliptic,
and regarded this day as the Change Station,
The Way Station, where a soul wanting to leave this world
could get off and go to another,
when those who died in the year
were finally released from this boundary.

Ramona, I've come this long journey
to bring you this news.
Your brother, whose *illness* was the voices he heard,
heard the Kachina Winds
calling to him
that Sunday morning
from the Singing Place.

    10.   Blood Brother, Ramon
I tell you of Isis walking through the desert
gathering the parts of Ra from the boiling sand.
I tell you in death
our dismembered parts, piece of flesh, piece of soul,
call to one another.
But when she is pregnant with him
she is condemned to give birth
in no month and in no year
as it is with those of us living.
We carry life and cannot be relieved of it.

Then we turn north to Gemini,
dance to the opposite Crossroads,
north to the nearest frontier of extra-galactic space,
the future to which we sail
in our little solar boat.

Beauty is the earth feeling itself, Ramona sings.

The Universe feels itself around us
in the mirror that is Earth.
We dance the bridge between the Fall and Winter Houses,
turn north over the red earth ground,
dance out the Great White Way beyond the flaming bars of the world
wearing bisnaza blossoms in our hair, twirling batons,
rearranging as we run in flickering darkness,
the events of his life.

We walk to and fro the end of the land,
our dark and light faces on the edge of the country.
We run to the bottom of the mountains,
root our souls in their violent bowels.
We dance the Cross of the Americas
formed by the Hopi migrations
whose center is the center of the world.

The Direction of the First World is West
Its name is Endless Space

The Direction of the Second World is South
Its name is Dark Midnight

The Direction of the Third World is East
Its color is red
which is the color of Love

The Direction of the Fourth World
is the World Complete

Now tied to the Wampum String that runs the song around
we face each other on the borderline.
Now South to the Source, now North again we turn
to the backdoor, icelocked, of the Twins

and listen to the Story riding up the World Axis,
a call from the Singing Place,
a breath, the color of love, blown on the pane:
your brother, a song across space
from the shore of the Fourth World

of Birdness
majestic in the Miracle Light
perched, beyond the blue of the flesh,
in the dwarfed oaks of your desert

whose wings are made of the dark widow clouds
whose feathers are edged with the mist of her tears
who holds in his claws
the present world and the world to come

11.
Ramona's Wedding Song: Pedro Rivera

He will come a year to your brother's death
when the Universe has turned again
into its deepest stardense frame

He will come from the Third World
which is the color of Love and your star, Antares
with its planet newly-discovered
revolving around it

The center of the world
will be found in you

and he will reach
through the dark weight of sorrowing cattle
leaning into your adobe
across the dirt floor
polished years ago with their blood

He will reach for you on the bed
across the man who has left you
to join a search party
for white men in Mexico

He will be no dark fantasy
but a man dark as the soft night to lie down in

whose language will be the sound
of a thousand mariachis at noon

His name will be of the River
flowing as this border
whose blood is the source of true nations
stranded souls will attempt to swim

And your name, Ramona Rivera
will drift as the rays of the sun
in its swift cool currents
south where the green rushes grow

When All Is Said And Done

In Ramona's dark trailer on the Mexico-Arizona border
I had to climb on top of him to find him.
My hands ran all over his body which I could only see
through the eyes in my fingers.

I looked at him the way the old woman in Bisbee
was looking at the people after the serenade that day.
She hung over her cane like the last, jealous leafing
of a tree whose trunk will last a hundred more years,
staring, in disbelief, at the people

the canyon-deep, vertical ruins her eyes
stared from, her mind blown in like the rainclouds
gathering on the border behind her

like Ramona's dead brother
rising as a bird from the oakstrewn floor

Then we drove away
across the morning desert crying.
The yellow cacti bloomed
in the red dry washes and draws.
Behind the cop hiding in the median grass
I saw Ramona's dead brother, a vaquero,
alone and palely loitering.

Midday out of Tucson it was too hot to go on.
We stopped at a cafe and drank beer.
Across the table, across the history of everything
he said *You and Ramona should be lovers.*
You understand each other and neither of you understand
the male ego.
In that small cowboy cafe I can still hear myself gasping
There's no such thing as the male ego, we all suffer
the human ego.

Starting out again, west, the temperature 117°,
west into the sun, dropping below the sea,
on our way home, the radio told the story
of the revolutionary couple
who kidnapped the famous heiress,
manacled and in waistchains, their last union,
bussed today to Chino
where once I lived in my Four-Bedroom
and down the suburban street
where housewives are thought to be left
I met Ramona
and Desdemona Gonzales.
When the prisoners cleaned the streets
the three of us swigged Tequila
and then put our bodies in the front yards
and mowed for them.

I said listen to the story of leaving for Ramona's years ago,
how I watched from the great anguish of the war
a doomed California Brown Pelican
rowing her prehistoric, now DDT lope
between the President's West Coast White House
on the edge of the sea
and the weeping juices of the setting sun

and then drove all night east
over this same road we are traveling now to the west
and saw arched in the sun as it rose
the fiery accident of two diesels

and I knew, sure as the old woman in Bisbee knew,
this is almost
incredible, this
is an omen

if only we could read, and he, weeping, begged me, please
can't we start over? which made me
weep, which made me lie
yes
but when I looked up from his shoulder
as we fell toward the Colorado

I looked up to an accident,
a car off in the wash on its back,
its wheels still spinning,
a woman cradling a man's ripped body in her lap
as if she has just given birth,
the couple's silhouette against the setting sun,
and we both knew
it is over

*...in 1952 and 1953 Kroeber traveled by car through Mojave country in the
company of an old Mojave man. Together they went to many of the places named
in a Mojave song cycle and epic account. Kroeber could locate many of the places
on a geodetic survey map.... He found that the distances traveled each day
according to the story worked out realistically on the ground, as did the
locations of the overnight stopping places or special spots for singing a long
series of songs. This is more interesting because the story had been
recounted to Kroeber in 1906 and for the further remarkable fact that it had,
the whole of it, been dreamed in the first place by its teller over a period
of many years.*

RAMON, THE COLORADO

    1. *Mojave*
You think of yourself as a national entity
freely crossing tribal boundaries.
You are a natural geographer
with a deep interest in landscape
and an accurate sense of both
position and distance.
Sometimes you travel as far as the Chumash on the coast,
the Yokuts of the San Joaquin.
You seek all the rivers.

    2. *Charon*
You meet me at the river of our state
where I leave him.
You will take me in a slow journey
across the desert to Ramona.

I look back, see him move north.
West, the violet hills lift and fall
where she lives. The color of her eyes.
Each day I think we will arrive, but nights
as we fall from the sun, she wakes, laughs,
and in the morning, recedes.

We sleep in the trailer your gold car pulls
parked in sagescrub lots of widows
who run gaspumps, rockshops, shrines
to their late husbands.
In a petrified forest we huddle around her bed to see
the haloed figures

a man, a woman, a child held between them

painted she explains from the steam of prickly pears she cans
by South America travelers 10,000 years ago
on rock that was moved here from the Grand Coulee
before it was dammed

3. Mojave
Dreams permeated the whole of your life.
There is a continuity between the earlier and later dreams.
They are additive, a story told in installments.
They are cumulative, dream added to dream, episode linked to esisode.

4. Charon
I wake on the floor beneath the kitchen table
to the whispers I heard as a child
when we camped at Dana Point.
My mother has moved to your bed.
I don't know where I am
or where you are, or my son, or my daughter.
The desert wind howls through Orion's frame,
through mesquite, ocotillo,
rocks our tin shelter, my lovers through me
like the dust that covers everything,
every tiny colored glass bead, the widow said,
I found on the Lewis and Clarke landing site
before the Columbia was dammed.
I'll spend the winter
polishing and stringing again.

5. Mojave
You need only sit or lie, turning the sun of your thoughts
inward where the dream lies waiting,
the dream you begin in your mother's womb.
Sometimes you leave her while she sleeps

and dream the rivers
the Colorado down from the Rockies, across the desert,
the Ramona underground all the way
from Canada to Baja.

6. Charon. My Orphan. My Country.
I can't forget the mystical islands of your feet
the small explosions of light
when you stepped to earth

nor the scars of your having been here.
Your crying comes from every geography.

The small girl falls dead of fright
when you gallop into the Rocky Mountain village
of a people who have never before seen
white men

in your miraculous double encirclement
of the uncharted Far West
a genuinely enlighted and religious man
that first time
you sought the mythical Buenaventura

dropping south from the Great Salt Lake
believed at first to be the Pacific Ocean
to the Mojave on the Colorado
who after *days like a holiday faire*
guide you within the hot Witches' Wind
west across the river, west through the fires
of Mojave hell to the pueblo of the angels
who, discerning *the first anglo overland
into our California,* imprison you, destroy your journals
before you escape, fleeing north
up the great central valley, seeking the pass
through the Range of Light
through which you are moving eight days
then out across the dark sedge and salt flats of Nevada
the place no river leaves
and your victorious return
to the Great Salt Lake

where with eighteen men you descend again
the route of the year before

> but somewhere this time in the grainy expanse
> in the unearthly light
> you lose your clear vision
> of God

> *Go back! Go back!* the eagle screams
> and spins above you as you watch
> twin fey Mojave deer
> walking as if asleep
> into the river

> *Dear girl,* you find yourself praying
> to that Rocky Mountain one,
> again and again,
> *be not afraid. Your death
> is quick, merciful.*

> *Dear God, forgive
> this door I open, this slow and sure death
> I bring*

to your favorite people, the copper-skinned,
straight-teethed, bare-chested
Mojave women, *dreamers and geographers,*
who hold it an honor to ask a white man
to sleep with them

but who this time,
midstream the Colorado, on rafts
they built for you, *ambush,*
killing ten of you

> a betrayal you almost understand
> for when you went into her, *Sahaykwisa,*
> you saw again the small girl
> dropping dead of fright beneath you
>
> and when suddenly she rolled you over
> you saw in her black eyes whirling all sides of you
> that she, *Sahaykwisa,*
> saw all that you portend.
> *When you enter me,* she said,
> *see my people dead.*

now swimming the Colorado River through your screaming men,
staggering with survivors in August
across the Mojave's unrelenting light
and heat, the Mojave untold distance, the stillness
of Mastamho, the psychotic fish-eagle Mojave God
she told you of, yeah, though you walk
through the valley of the shadow of death
with your God, *who is not mystery, who is not strange visions,*
you understand you will survive
for you see too clearly your death by Comanches
many years from now at the head of the Cimarron

to the Pueblo of Angels, turning this time unseen
north up the Great San Joaquin
but missing the lit passage through the Range of Light
and so trapping the mystical rivers later known
as the Kern, the King, the San Joaquin, the Merced,
the Tuolemne, the Stanislaus, the Mokelumne, the American,
the Yuba, the Feather, the Sacramento, the Russian,
the Eel, the Mad, the Trinity, the Redwood,
the Smith, the Klamath, the Roque

until you are so far north
you are the first whites overland to Oregon
and all your men are massacred
by the Kelawatset on the Umpqua.

7. *Mojave*
She told you the origin of death
was set by Matavilye
who decided the people had to be mortal
lest the earth should become so crowded
the people would have to void
their excreta on each other.

Matavilye was in the primal house
when he resolved to die
so as to set precedent.
He was ill at the time and felt the need to defecate.
Rising from his bed, he headed toward the door
and on passing near his daughter
he touched her genitals.

Was she angry because he touched her?
she, lover, Sahaykwisa, *Mojave tattooed face beneath you*
teasing ahwe-nyevedi,
Or because when he did so,
now bare-chested Mojave girl on top of you,
he wished to void his stools?

His daughter in that moment became the first witch.
She dived into the ground, emerged
exactly under her father
and by swallowing his excreta
bewitched him. Shortly thereafter
Matavilye died as he intended
thereby bringing death into the world.

When they cremated him, she concluded,
waving her hands crazily across your heart
as if to ward off the ahwe-nyevedi,
the phallic foreign ghost illness,
Coyote, leaping over Badger and Racoon,
the shortest persons present,
grabbed his heart and ran away with it.
And so as punishment, Coyote became,
and she told you this as warning,
a foolish, insane tramp of the desert.

8. *Charon*
The season changes.
The wind chills. The mountains blue.
The interstate closes due to the migration of cockroaches.
On the high desert the tree of Joshua waits,
his arms uplifted.

We wait in the Borax Soap and Gem Cafe
beneath posters of our Hollywood leaders.
In yesterday's papers on the counter I find
de Vaca In A Vanishing Geography.

The power of maintaining life in others
lives within each of us
and from each of us does it recede
when unused.

It is concentrated power.
If you are not acquainted with it,
O my majesty,
you can have no idea of what it is like,
what it portends or the ways
in which it slips from one.

A book of poems printed without the poet's name.
An eagle soaring the cover.
The copyright says
anticopy, to avoid
the commodity spectacle.

Suddenly a crazed old miner cries out,
his white cataracts flashing
like sudden neon

The Colorado no longer flows to the sea!
The Grand Canyon is filling up with rocks!
They're gonna blow us to hell and back
the whole stinkin mess, just you watch, Baby,
even you and your pretty face.

In the dream we're on the bus to Long Beach.
Enormous oilships float on polluted waters
beneath Signal Hill.
The sky is oily, the palmtrees uprooted, the land torn.
Delighted, I shout to you, *Look!*
my birthplace!

You are embarrassed, apologetic.
I understand then
we are on our way to another dope deal.
I ride beside you, my hand on your thigh,
mortified once again, by my terrible innocence,
pondering which drug you have for sale.

I'm in a room with two of you.
Blood shoots like a fountain
from my vagina.
You have wounded me enough, I plead.
But you both prepare for rape.

I'm running in the streets
down from your prison in the mountains.
Filthy, in a ragged dress, blood pours
from my wounded eye.
My parents, parked in the alley, wait for me.
Someone is on the other side of the river.

Ramon, was it you who killed her?
Is that why you left?

You climb the sage, the river, canyon, time and the clouds.
You pull me down in fields.
As if birth had never found you
and death could never end you
you spill hot milk on my belly.

The children are armor plated
ascending from the gulf.
The fathers are hooded, driving Gabrieleno slaves
with mission bells from the west.
The wagon trains are fused in the eastern light
of grandmothers

all coming to find you, Mojave, half-breed, dark beloved
in the land.

> 9. *Mojave*
> *As shaman you could cause the soul*
> *to leave the body and be lost.*
> *You could as well search out the lost soul*
> *and return it to its body.*
> *A person or a country, you said,*
> *cannot long survive*
> *the loss of soul.*

> 10. *Coeur 'd Alene. Ducktown.*
Seventy years/Hidden, the hangman/In the navel, or/An eye in the oblivion/
Of an instantaneous Being.../

We ride away west many years later
from the bottom of the land
toward the late ruins, the date palms, the Salton Sea.
I buy polished garnet for my mother,
three for a quarter.
You tell me of '33
when you jumped freights from Tennessee
to catch the wheat harvest in Idaho.
She says you told her the first day you met
the most beautiful place you had ever seen
was Coeur d' Alene.
Someday, you vowed
you would take her there.

I see you again on Mt. Wilson
seated on a granite boulder above Los Angeles,
rolling a cigarette in your thick fingers.
The basin and sea are world-enormous behind you.
I am five, *Santana*, the hot Witches' Wind, inside me.

We eat cake Mama poured into a heart
then baked with minature redhot candyhearts.
My father's birthday is Valentine's Day!
I shout to the millions below.
Day of the heart, Daddy, day of the lover, Ramon,
the day birds choose their mates
for the year.

Now we visit mining towns, take the tour
beneath a collapsed mountain.
I see you looking for your father, the hardrock miner.
A stope is a step-like excavation of the mine,
the girl guide tells us,
a drift is 7x7 and through it passes the train.

The company doesn't care about the minerals.
Individual miners carry them out, garnet, ruby,
silver, even gold.

Outside, the world is light, sky
makes us cry. We drink Mendocino burgundy
over the Land of the Dead
where the Mojave go
under the bed of the Colorado.
I ask you about the bridge you built
across the Los Angeles River before I was born.
You hold your left wrist with your right hand
count the missing beats.
I see the place enormous pain
has carved in me for you, the Colorado diverted,
her mouth full of salt.
Tears rim, spill from your eyes
when my brother is mentioned.
Your eyes, Daddy, I've always been told
are mine.

The setting sun slowly defines the world
into deeper burgundy. Then the world
like Osiris, the Many Eyed who dreams the rivers,
is lost.

When in the boat of Ra
Isis rises in her fullest search,
we speak at last of my brother.
And then his ex-wife. We speak
of my sister, her ex-husband.
I tell you of my men, the ones who have so offended you.
The stories are impossible to understand,
but even so, we speak timidly
of love
for these missing persons.

I tell you everyone I know has one of these stories,
the end of love, the rivers dammed, the earth mined,
the gems carried out to make the bomb.
Once I took a vow never to be a poet, but now,
this manmade desert back of us, this 200th anniversary,
how can I not polish and string
these beads of blood and light?

I read you my poem
of your hometown.
I avoid Ramon, the sexual imagery,
the time you hit me. Even so,
I'm shocked. How could I have written this?
Where did I get these stories?
I discover you did not know
your father was a hangman.

I must be wrong.
I'll cut it out, erase it, it is not
important to anything now. You protest
we don't know for certain and why
is it so sad? Crying

I tell you of Uranus, the Father myth,
that love was born from the severed part.
I tell you your hometown is just symbolic
of what could happen

the whole earth
without trees, without flowers, without grass, or birds,
the way it's supposed to be, our children will think, plutonium

splashed   blood-red   rain-rotted   tree-split   body-ripped   hillskulls

who swam in a river of cupric chloride
and copperheads
who has no memory

you, Daddy, who tell me now for the first time
of your boyhood

Pa always planted a garden, no matter how poor we were.
Ma planted fruit trees.

You stood in this greenery
as on an island, feeling safe.
The sunsets were more beautiful than even Ramona,
the earth exposed, you could see it

color like jello splashed on jagged peaks
There was beauty
like Arizona in Tennessee.

11. *Ramona, La Reina*

I know my archetype
the straw-bleached, boozy matron
the desert hag
who rode on top of me
those first nights of puberty
pulling from my sleeping girlbody
orgasm after orgasm.

La Llorona, La Chingada, Sahaykwisa,
Aphrodite. She is the monster adult
I had to grow into, she who orders Eros
to addict the innocent Psyche
with an irresistible passion
for the basest of men.

Father. Mother. Friend. Earth,
have mercy on me, *Ramon.*
I am trying to be a poet
but much of what I do
is like Nijinsky
jacking-off into a scarf
before his premier audience.

My desert beginning, my bookless lore
are not easy countries.
I am overly large
in this small scrub.
I write these poems but cannot
for all my heart and excessive will
turn around quick enough
to stop myself
singing in the strange way.

Nor am I ever to forget
or to forgive
the suffering my words bring.

12. *Mojave*

The nighsky rises and blows
the riverine call of nightingale.
Joshua, bathed in moon, beckons me
to the high horizon.

Blind Orion runs in place
to catch his eyes in the fallen sun
while the comet falls through him
heavy and swift as the songs of the daughters
calling from the old reedboats on the river.

I move into his grotesque arms, carefully turn
within the hairy thorns, the moon's shaft,
to face the east, the land I've just traversed.

A red mist rises off the dry riverbed.
A lizard humps, hunches at my feet.
The border falls away to cloud, sky,
an old woman geographer dreaming
Colorado, *so broad, so wide, so deep, passing*
without sound.

And suddenly it is you,
O, my majesty,
playing with me, humming
through your vegetable arms.

Part IV
HEARTSEA

Coyote, ululating on the hill,
Is it my fire that disturbs you so?
Or the memories of long ago
when you were a man
roaming the hills?

Jaime de Angulo

Everything shall perish except your heart.

The Sioux

Los Angeles
The Pornographer: The mind in which we all participate.

1.
We drive out of the drought-seared land of the north.
The news is of two skeletons in a car
uncovered in Clear Lake.
Water so low, wives
who have been looking for their husbands
nine Christmases,
find them.

2.   The Howling Beast On The Borderline Which Separates You From Me
Beneath the ancient city of Yagna
on Christmas Eve
we meet again.
In your windowless basin,
a tomb that fits you perfectly,
your stiff thin body
breaks on me.
Your hands
like rotting slats of an old wooden fence
break to let me out.

The great mystery
is how you hid your face from me.
All the years I lived with you
I could not see you. From your breasts,
like Isis from Ra, I cut your name
and planted it in my own.
My eyes put you in all the land,
but still, I cannot see.

I've wandered the country
to shed your million faces
looking from the windows of my body.
Our small graves litter the land,
parts of you, parts of me.
Over them I have inscribed

Zorro, Coyote, Amon-Ra

He Who Hides His Name
He Who Hides His Heart
He Who Hides His Womb

Still, the northern side of your face
is lost in the San Gabriels
that shadow this town.

I come to the rainy street.
Leaves of rubber trees, carob seed
blow against us.
Coyotes circle the city singing your name.
Our son and daughter circle us, breaking.
They have never seen me cry.
They move away, stand apart
like ancient skeletons
as if my tears have drowned them.

3.   The Ones Who Think Jesus Is Santa Claus As A Young Man
We walk downtown for gifts.
Angels are seeds.
You can hear their moans
soaked in asphalt
the black sleep
burst from the ground,
between us and the town.

Angel's Flight is gone.
The Anglos of the daylight are gone,
and now, nights, Christmas Eve, 6th and Hill,
the old Pueblo falls back
to the ancient faces of Yagna.

Mouths red and perfectly formed
float as canoes down the street.
Cheeks that are mountain ranges
drift through faces
like great faults of continent moving west.

I follow you, drifting through their faces,
their Indian streetbones, whole blocks
of sperm and silent blood spewing from lips,
stories spilling like drunks
around the bus station

of this last town

Your thin body moves through it.
I keep an eye on you. Ashamed, I spy on you.
Your hands clutch air: *you* could always hold it.
I keep your face between me and them,
the blinding Sun between me and the Universe.

I see how they honor your scars, your male disguises.
As a boy in Dogtown
they knew Zorro as Lobo,
Lobo as Coyote and you learned
to mask yourself in their dark myths.
You learned in these streets
soon there will be no white people.

Gifts are being wrapped
from the country south of here,
messages in little boxes.
I have jewelry I have gold I hardly knew
a war was going on

Your brow bends around the movie marquee,
pornography: the only thing you love.
You raise your hand to shade your eyes from the neon glare
and separate into stained-glass figures
that float north and east to the hills
where your kind roams, elusive of all cages.

Illusive Coyote! Trickster God of Turtle Island!
Slick and cool Trickster God of Los Angeles,
your laughter erupts from some tree, rains down
seduces them, seduces me, the semen
I taste just looking at you.

I step through centuries and see
the savior was a boy
who never brought his body to the world,
an infant withering on a tree
sucking everything, light, lovers, the earth
into his small knotted body.

In the shadow of the Hall of Justice where we first met
you a prisoner and I a young mother
who left her son crying in the car
to visit you on Christmas Eve

I see again the Wanted posters
with your faces, your many names

Zorro, Coyote, Amon-Ra

He Who Hides His Name
He Who Hides His Heart
He Who Hides His Womb

I hammer a list of your gravesites
on a bankwall

From the store
where they barter
I have jewelry I have gold
the music like a strange wind

o, come let us adore Him

4.

You drive the Golden State Freeway
your hands posed on the wheel like rusted rifles.
I'm crying again what of love? What of
forgiveness? You cry again
the absolute desperado, don't pin me down

We drive through pyramids of wrecked and rusted cars,
death-cracked, rain-rotted skulls, buffalo
bones, our passage as hunters
through the obsolete land.

On Vermont Avenue
a white-haired black man prays on a bus bench

hands clasped before his face
the tree lit in the window behind him

As we turn onto Pico
a police car, the California bear prowling its doors,
pulls up to him

a gun in the scarred hands, oh
we were almost
great
brave in our narrow pride

your hands like scar tissue
your hands like old trophies
your hands like dead bear claws
your hands like dead decorated trees
your hands like old wooden crosses

5.

You close your eyes, pretend to touch me.
Where you find your old slashes
you draw back scared.
Your hands stop six inches from my body, your scars.
Your hands grow a gun instead.

Your American heart grows scars and stops.
The one inside grows scared and stops.
Everything stops.
You will not come closer.
You will not come into
the real country.

6.   Amon/Amon-Ra

I learned to be a man from you.
You did not learn to be a woman from me.

I learned to be a hunter from you.
You did not learn to be a lover from me.

I became a soldier with you
in the fight against the war,
acts I still cannot reveal.

I became a soldier
what every girls knows
she never has to be

what every boy knows
he must automatically be

In you I overcame the greatest fears
In you I hid my womb
In you I hid my heart

For you I killed our babies
For you I would do it still

the heartwork
the wombwork
the axe-and gun work

O, husband, we were almost
great
but in me, you did not learn
to be a mother
In me, you still know
your greatest fears

You glory in your role
the uncommitted killer
your trickster gun
your perfect wombless solitude

and then in the mode of your walk
across the land
to take the curse off
like the Child of this night
you become what is wounded, destroyed

    7.   Christmas Day
I stay in bed all day. Fever.
You are gone. Sometimes I wake
to birds
chittering in avocado trees
an animal skin on the wall
a young child crying in the street

I dream of three wild bears
flying over the Sierras.
I dream you wear a wine-red shirt
and seagulls nest in your black curls.
Your eye is the light of the moon.
You wear five earrings in your right ear
but none in the small pierced hole of your left.

253

Beneath your beautiful hands the sea
lifts and falls

A way opens at my feet.
I go down the many colored lights
the steps into Earth.
The years fly up in my face

as your hands, like crosses,
take me up from the sofa and dance me
in the small shack.
Beyond your hair the sea lifts and falls
against the end of continent
where we walk again
through the 12,000 year old Maliwu cemetery
being bulldozed for a trailer park.

A man on a tractor reaches down and hands me
a pelvic bone.
I've carried it with me
as I've carried your body
ever since.

It is my jewelry, it is my gold.
It is the real thing,
a 12,000 year old American hunter

or woman, her ancient house
through which the people have come
into now

How do I let you go?

How do I lift the tormented architecture of your body
off mine, the live coal you put in me,
the secret things you did in me?
What do I do with this love you have rejected

that I fear is all that protects you,
your cold, scarred body
from death?

8.   Angel's Flight
The moon is caught in Saturn's rings,
retrogrades, the backward motion.
Your children and I head north
but at the Grapevine, travelers are lost
in drifting snow. The passes close.
So we come to your mother's house,
to this town, *Ojai*, the Chumash word for nest,
in the mountain refuge for condors
who will soon be extinct.

The wild mountain passes of this place are always
shocking, as if explaining the strange city
they enter. In a time when the earth was still soft
it was said the land grew ever to the south
and the first people, naked, lonely and cold,
kept following it.

I keep following you.
You taught me this land. You are the land.
This is the bed your body folded around me.
All night I listen to the new year's rain
throw itself against the house I found for you,
and against the house next door of the last Chumash family.
I listen to the sobs tear from my body
beneath pillows, mountains, asphalt,
a bird downed in a storm, tortured
in the small cage of my ribs.
Your beautiful mother breathes too deeply, cries out.
Your son and daughter sleep on the floor.
She speaks to you.
He groans in his new voice.
I listen.

How did we do it?
How do we bear it?
How do we live now?

I turn on the light and read
but the beat of the rain is too strong.
Behind the livid hieroglyphs a woman
I don't see is on the horizon of the desert, screaming.
She tears her body against the blue hills, throws
the pieces to the coyotes who surround her
who are closing in
until, at last, through the downpour, I see her

some terrible forsaken angel of the basin, crazed,
lamenting endlessly the loss of her lover

until I find my body dead
in the asphalt-whorled basin of the world
a man's face floating
in every drowned cell

until I hear again
the Earth crying

you must love me
as much as I love you

until I step through centuries and see
I am as guilty as he,
betrayer of the Body, the Earth, Marriage and Love,
consort, abettor, accomplice, partner, mate, the congregation
gathered on the shore
to watch her drown

until, I, victim,
see in you, killer,
myself, slave and slavemaster,
and understand at last
the hatred against women

until I in young soldiers see
the mother's betrayal,
she, in whom he should have been safe,
forgetting birth, hands him over
to the bloodstained hands of the father,
to murder or be murdered

until I in young daughters see
the mother's betrayal,
she, in whom she should have been safe,
forgetting birth, hands her over,
a bloodstained spoil of war,
to the father

until I know again
to love
is not to transcend the horrors I have known
or the earth
I have never loved

but to know and contain them
within my body

to remember
our dis-membered parts
and then
to survive
this memory

though my eyes are gouged out
to *see*

though my tongue is cut out
to *sing*

until I come through the center of the Mystery
which is you
which is sex, which is
Love and see
our only chance,
man, husband, father, brother, son, country,
female, is to become
in this late century
on this nuclear brink
Woman

O Isis, to sculpt
after the body has been found
the missing testicles,
to rise, O Refugee, out of the shadow of his damned city,
to rise, O Chumash, into the mountains a great condor,
to lift the dead from the small water,
to let him go. The year is over. Two hundred years.
The Earth comes back.

Come back. As I must.
Rise out of his hands that are obsolete guns,
rise into the ranges and passes
be the flying bear of your dreams,
feel the great groaning weight of the wings,
move east from the Ventura Plain into the Santa Monicas
over these rare, east-west mountains of the continent,
look down, see the triumphant peaks, the faultlines,
the deserts and valleys circling and whirling the great basin,
the Gabrielenos, the blue dancing lovers
on this ever-expanding Southland that opens now so wide
to this water pouring from the borders of your sanity, the sky
weeping repentant rain over the barriers
between the desert and the sea
over the jeweled lights of the basin
over the bodies of the barrios
over the barrio of his soul
over the palos verdes and the palisades
over the islands of the sea
over the Lone Woman of St. Nicolas Island
over the grave of Cabrillo
over the coastline of your birthplace
over the mother who drowned herself
over your mother in the garden
who understands at last
what your grandmother is saying
over Ramon strewn in pieces on Jacinto
over Ramona who lies around him in thought over Mexico
the rain

the rain pouring through the freeways
the parking lots, the shopping centers, the housing tracts,
the car accidents, the nuclear sites,

the rain, our human water, the Earth
crying

until I am washed away of my covers
until Chumash I am washed away of my sorrow   .
until Condor I am snow over the sea

until flying bear I am snowing in the passes
until white buffalo I am sinking into blue mountains
until female I am filling the dry wells and reservoirs
until male I am moving granite boulders down the ravished river beds
until daughter I am rushing the arroyos and flooding
until son I am washing clean the bloodied alleys and pavements

until Mother I am water in the mouths of thirsty people
until Father I am the water that bathes their wondrous bodies

until Lover and Earth I am the great plates of the continent moving west
the land that ever expands to the south
Ramona rising from Ramon in the east

until the sea itself flows from my veins
and the blue love of the sky
pulls the whole sea from me
and pours me

                    as blue living light

on all the ridges of the world
I have always loved

until, *alcatraz*, off-shore by islands hidden in the blood,
jewels and miracles, I am the Pelican:
the consumed heart between the White House and the Sun
the human between the male and the female

buoyed for the moment on my barren coffin, my soft-shelled eggs,
with only love for hope
look back onto the whole country, its lethal tide
its love of death
its hatred of love
and warn you

Albion-Elk-Mendocino-Port Townsend-Ashland
1975-1982

258

NOTES

Throughout the poem, *Hard Country*, when I have not used the tribal name, I have used the term "Indian." As has been noted, all the contemporary usages, *Native American, indigenous people, Amerindian*, etc., are European. "When Columbus was in the Caribbean he was not looking for a country called India. Europeans were calling that country Hindustan in 1492. Columbus called the tribal people he met 'Indio,' from the Italian *in dio*, meaning *in God.*"   Russell Means.

At the further risk of misunderstanding, a note on my evocation of American Indian cultures, in imagery, story, and vision, seems in order. *Hard Country* is written from the perspective of having shed the colonial, racist and sexist attitudes of our literature. Though I also evoke the European cultures that are my heritage too, I am mainly interested in the American continents, in American gods and goddesses, myths, stories, geography and history evolved from the land and the people who have lived on this land for untold centuries. I am interested in the universality and synthesis of certain myths but it is as an American Isis that I wander the land in search of the lover strewn in pieces across it, buried in it, rather than as Eygptian or Greek, or European. I have named her variously, Ramona, Santana, Sacajawea, Sasquatch, Marilyn, Donna, Nga-my, Emanuelle, Lilith, Daughter of Albion, Rose of Sharon, The Linga Sharira, Amazon, Loretta, Cinderella, Sappho, Black Buffalo Woman, Eliza, Lady of the Lake, Mama, Evangeline, fata morgana, La Llorona, La Chingada, Sahaykwisa, Eve, Psyche, I Am, Old Woman Geographer, Angel, Charon, etc.—particularly, Charon in the sense of the ferry person evoked to help us across this terrible River of Lethe on this interminable journey to the New World. My apologies are offered here for any misunderstandings that this evocation may cause among the people of this land whose cultures have been seized so ruthlessly in the past. As I have always done I ask the Great Spirit, the Muse, Psyche in the Land, to forgive my ignorances, my excesses, my failings, and then I ask that it continue to open, to reveal to me and to all who genuinely seek, the correct path of this urgent quest.

PART 1, HEADSTONE

Headstone, I: *Headstone*

3. "The ancient light of the ground," Wendell Berry.
   "Eight days down the Tennessee..." The Needham-Arthur Diary, 1673.

5. "And the Mississippi flowed backwards..." *The New Madrid*, **Missouri Earthquakes**, December 1811-January 1812.
   "Before I was born my body..." Carolyn Forche, *Burning the Tomato Worms*.

9. The Linga Sharira, the Long Body of the Solar System, the structure of our galaxy, the ancient "Crossroads of Time and the Universe," "when the Gods call for us," occurs between November 18-23 each year. A further explanation of the Linga Sharira, the ancient Hindu name for the Milky Way, "the form on which our physical body is molded," can be found in *Arizona*, 9.

10. "The postcards of Ducktown, Tennessee, give only a faint idea of the devastation which goes on. Imagine an area fifty square miles so poisoned by the fumes of the copper plant that everything is killed off and the earth itself made to look like a convulsive red scar! Grand to see in a way, like a Dore illustration of the **Inferno**. But what a place for people to live..." Henry Miller to Anais Nin, October, 1940.

17. "The entire movement of 'Confessional Poetry' may be said to have commenced on the evening of November 18, 1953, when during a piano concert W.D. Snodgrass scribbled on the back of his program lines which eventually became the beginning of **Heart's Needle**:

>   child of my winter, born
>   when the soldiers died
>   on the ice hills, when I was torn..."

This citation from Steven Gould Axelrod's **Robert Lowell: Life and Art** was a major inspiration for the poem **Headstone**, particularly the section *November 18, 1953: The Linga Sharira*. I give it here under the Linga Sharira title to suggest still another perspective on the much-maligned term "Confessional Poetry."

Headstone, II: *American Alchemy:* for my children, Danny and Shawn

I am indebted to Marcelene Brogli, organizer of the Vietnamese/Cambodian refugee camp's Family Planning Clinic at Camp Pendleton, Oceanside, California, of whom my sister and I were guests in August, 1975.

Part I: *Ramona*
1. I am indebted to Jane Fonda for this story.

2. This poem is based on an interpretation of the ancient Chinese classic, **Fusang**. See Henriette Mertz, **Pale Ink** (Chicago, The Swallow Press).

3. Helen Hunt Jackson, **Ramona**. See also her **Century of Dishonor**.

Part II: *Hard Now Against the Man: Female Problems*

"The American part of the war had begun in Danang..." Dennis Troute, "The Last Days of Saigon," *Harper's* July, 1975.

The "chorus" throughout Part II is from a poem inspired by Margaret Duras' film, *Hiroshima Mon Amour*.

1. v. "Ramona, come closer..." Bob Dylan.

PART II, HEADLAND

Headland, I: *Ramon/Ramona*

I Was Born Coming to the Sea: for my mother, March 27, 1978.

Headland, II: *Bicentennial*

Visions of a Daughter of Albion: for Loretta Manill

1. "My soul can find/no well of clear water," Ed Dorn, *For the Union Dead in Alabama.*

6. "Shame to live in a land..." Bob Dylan.

8. Robert Duncan, *A Poem Beginning with a Line by Pindar* (epigraph and quotes in text).

9. H.D., *The Islands.*

10. "Break open my heart," barry eisenberg.

You Leave: for Nada and Fred.

PART III, HEARTLAND

Seattle: The versification is from S.K. Webb, **American HXATAL** (Austin, Place of Herons Press, 1978).

Kerouac and Monroe on Kalaloch: For Michael Daley.

Oregon, 6: Adapted from the journal of Jesse A. Applegate.

Leaving Boise: Retreat: for Leonard Cirino.

"What lays waste my heart..." Kiva.

2. *"Califia, the Amazon,* the mythic California woman:" the reference is to the popular 1510 Spanish novel by Garcia Rodriguez Ordonez de Montalvo, from which the state of California derives its name.

3. Adapted from Benjamin Capps, **The Great Chiefs** (New York, Time-Life Books).

4. "Mrs. Pound was a beautiful woman..." H.D., **End To Torment** (New York, New Directions), p. 22.

5. Adapted from Mary Welsh Hemingway, **How It Was** (New York, Knopf).

Utah: This poem is based on theological tenets of the Church of Latter Day Saints as I understand them. *Lamanites:* The Mormon term for American Indians. "The heart of America": a sign at the south entrance declares the heart of America to be Yellowstone.

Yellowstone:

6. Adapted from "A Video Conversation with Robert Curry," Peter Berg, Peter Coyote, "Planet Drum."

10. "I kissed goodbye the howling beast..." Bob Dylan.

Wyoming:

"They crossed the Continental Divide..." Capps.

1. Testimony, The Sand Creek Massacre Investigation, November 29, 1869.

2. Thomas Marquis, **Keep the Last Bullet for Yourself** (Two Continents, 1976).

4. Capps, **The Great Chiefs**. "And the boy Crazy Horse..." adapted from Mari Sandoz, **Crazy Horse, The Strange Man of the Oglalas** (Nebraska, University of Nebraska Press).

5. The white buffalo myth: Barry Lopez, "Buffalo," **Winter Count** (New York, Scribners).

6. "In the name of what God, what happened, what thing," Sam Hamill, **Sam Hamill's Triada** (Port Townsend, Washington: Copper Canyon).

7. "The consumed heart/the setting sun," Robin Blaser.

8. "Pales with your water hearts," Thomas Roberdeau, *Tracks*.

Crazy Horse: Crazy Horse's story, as told in the extraordinary biography by Mari Sandoz, is that of a mystic warrior, that is, a medicine man who because of the times in which he lived became a warrior and a leader of his people. His story is equally a great love story and a story of the psychological effects of genocide. In my poem I am struck by a number of "dream adaptations" from Sandoz's book which I was reading on March 25, 1979. The ominous presence of the *black marriage robe* (a dominant article throughout the book): due to the political circumstances of the Plains tribes at the time, Crazy Horse was unable to marry the woman of his choice, *Black Buffalo Woman*; he married instead *Black Shawl Woman*, to whom he was a devoted husband. "I braid grass stems into his light hair": though full-blooded Oglala (for seven generations anyway) Crazy Horse had blond hair; his childhood name was Curly (this was one of the reasons he was called Strange). "I will grieve through seven generations...": The oral tradition of the Oglalas, their history and stories and geneaology are brought forth seven generations. "I pull him on the back of my horse...": In the last great battles, Crazy Horse was saved twice by Cheyenne women warriors. "On the Holy Road...": The Holy Road was the first white man's road through the North Platte Territory of the Sioux. "I am careful not to hold his arms down ...": Crazy Horse's warrior vision was that he was invincible, indeed invisible, unless one of his own people held down his arms. Needless to say, when he was stabbed to death in 1876, in a betrayal most likely instigated by No Water, the jealous husband of Black Buffalo Woman, Little Big Man was holding down his arms.

Plainsongs. for Meridel Le Sueur, for *Corn Village*.

1. Makoshika: for Barry Lopez who told me of the Crows.

Hard Country. for Celo V'ec. I am also indebted for imagery, ideas and tone to Francis Parkman, **The Oregon Trail**, and to Mei-Mei Berssenbrugge's "Pat Rat Steve," most notably the lines: "Sometimes a mirror where the hall turns/will show...", "Each night the sun slides out below the clouds/and lights a section of the rainbow...", "At twilight...grows into a large violet/shape...", "Like a violin without breath," "Wishbones...knotholes depicting the galaxies...", "She'd been dreaming about her death...", "The way the sound enters her...the blood inside your ear, or an urge to go look at the plain/your back to the town..." and "A flood plain where the river swerves...".

Detroit I: "Children goose stepping in place," Bill Bradd.

Detroit II, Huron: Adapted from an essay by Richard Grossinger, *Solar Journey* (Los Angeles, Black Sparrow Press).

Tennessee:

"Until they came..." Jack Hirschman.

4. The Needham-Arthur Diary.

Looking for the Melungeon: "In a past life, Love..." Loretta Manill, *Big River*. "I could be/Japanese," Sylvia Plath.

It'll Be a Bad Winter if Screech Owls Sound like Women Crying: for Billy Jean Hicks.

Song of Songs: The Lady in the Lake: for Geneva.

The quoted lines in this poem are largely from the Song of Solomon.

7. "Killing is a form..." Rilke, **Sonnets to Orpheus** (II, eleven).
"Who'll show a child..." Rilke, **Duino Elegies**, The Fourth Elegy.
"Murderers are easily understood..." Ibid.
"For it is not so much to know the self/as to know it as it is known/by galaxy and cedar cone"—A.R. Ammons.

Mother: for my mother. Secondly this poem is for Penelope Ann Clarke Yeats Hilde Kaufman, my recently found cousin, "lost in World War II," and for her two daughters, Sally and Nancy.

Appalachian Song: "I see a road inside myself/and on it I am running": Gerard Malanga, *The Edge of Vision*. "Call my name in the act of love," Michael Larrain, from poem of the same title.

Travels with Charley: "Who for her hunger shall I say..." Leonard Cohen.

Austin: The Making of a Boy: Some adaptations from Doris Kearns, **Lyndon Johnson and the American Dream** (New York, Harper and Row).

6. The Linga Sharira: see *Arizona*, 9.

Petrified Forest: For Joy Harjo.

Arizona: "Every year..." Frank Waters, **The Book of the Hopi** (New York, Ballantine).

2. "The Earth with her bars..." Jonah 2:6.

7. "I kissed goodbye..." Bob Dylan.

9. The Linga Sharira (The Long Body of the Dream, The Long Body of the Solar System, The Line of God, etc.), Rodney Collins, **The Theory of Celestial Influence** (New York, Samuel Weiser), pp. 10-14. Giorgio de Santillana and Hertha von Dechend, **Hamlet's Mill** (Boston, Gambit), pp. 239-41. P.D. Ouspensky, **Tertium Organum** (New York, Vintage), p. 46. Helena Blavatsky, **The Secret Doctrine**.

Ramon, The Colorado: The Mojave excerpts are adapted from Theodora Kroeber and Robert F. Heizer, **Almost Ancestors, The First Californians** (San Francisco, Sierra Club) and George Devereux, **Mohave Ethnopsychiatry: The Psychic Disturbances of an Indian Tribe** (Washington, Smithsonian Institute).

6. The story is of Jedidiah Smith. I am particularly indebted to Devereux for his

wonderful accounts of the Mojave lesbian, Sahaykwisa.

10. "Seventy years/Hidden..." Kenneth Rexroth, *Dative Haruspices*

PART IV, HEARTSEA

In this section, HEARTSEA, and throughout the poem **Hard Country**, I am greatly indebted to Richard Slokin, **Regeneration through Violence, The Mythology of the American Frontier, 1600-1860** (Connecticut, Wesleyan University Press).

Los Angeles:

"The pornographer..." Susan Griffin, **Pornography and Silence** (New York, Harper & Row).

2. "The howling beast..." Bob Dylan.

3. "The ones who think Jesus is Santa Claus..." from a poem recited in a film produced by Lena Wertmueller.

4. Maliwu: the Chumash place name.

7. "A way opens/at my feet. I go down/the night-lighted mule steps into earth..." Galway Kinnell, *The Book of Nightmares*.

8. "Until, off-shore, by islands hidden in the blood/jewels and miracles..." Charles Olson, **The Maximus Poems**.

ACKNOWLEDGEMENTS

The poem *Hard Country* would be an entirely different poem if it had not been for the inestimable influence of each member of my family, to whom the work is dedicated, and either directly or indirectly, of the following:

Michael Daley, Celo V'ec, Albion Moonlight, Ramona Rivera, Loretta Manill, Kathi Black, Susan Evans Stein, Wallace Berman, Jack Hirschman, Kristen Wetterhahn, Charles Hodges, Leonard Cirino, Kiva, Carolyn Forche, Richie Peckner, barry eisenberg, Feather Potenza, Bill Bradd, Devreaux Baker, Thomas Roberdeau, Gordon Black, Luke Breit, Liz Helenchild, Karol Kay Hope, Nancy Littleriver, Cynthia Frank, Curt Berry, Mary Norbet Korte, Duane BigEagle, Patricia Hamilton, Carl Kopman, Alice and Douglas Chouteau, Sandy Soen, Diana Dailey, Rick Sutherland, Marjorie, Nancy Curtis, Judith Tannenbaum, Efrain Correal, Mary Correal, Russ and Carol McDonnel, Carl Moore, Bob Avery, Judy Mahan, Tim Conner, Karin Faulkner, John Fremont, Scot Crogan, Bill and Shilla Lamb, Pat McKay, Ruth Bower, Lyn Hejenian, Caroline Allen, Liselotte Glozer, Paul McHugh, Betty Barber, Eliza Hicks, Beth Bosk, George Sanchez, Zida O'Brian, Nick Wilson, Don Shanley, Peter Lit, Monica and Jay Frankston, Gerry Colby, Sherry Thomas, Harriet Bye, Deseree Taylor, Conrad Schmidt, Biff Rose, Leah Leopold, Lydia Rand, Joanne Bochner, Tacie Lowe, Daniel Fernandez, Louie Callas, Richie and Catherine Rosenbaum, John Chamberlin, Kathy O'Grady, John and Nan Wetzler, Judy Williamson, Danita Rose, Roy Michaels, Kay Madden, Larry Madden, Ferenz, Barbara, Jude, Alma Villanueva, Wilfredo Castano, Philip Suntree, Susan Suntree, Dale Pendell, Steve Sanfield, Eugene Ruggles, Jim Cody, Barry Lopez, Sy Baldwin, Doreen Stock, Susan Raphael, River, Greg Donovan, Robert Greenway, Richard Alcott, Jeromy Pohl, Marnie Purple, Jim Masten, Jack Moyer, Wayne Howard, Ron and Vickie McBride, Juan Louis Dammert, Walter King, Tom Coroneos, Barbara Bodner, Jack and Jill Dowd, Denise and Stephanie Potenza, Brandice Hope, Annie Shepard, Windy Need, Corey Winn, Amelia Garcia, Jim Forstner, Tony Marx, Nancy Marx, Bob and Sue Winn, Clay Pennebaker, Judith Greenberg Azrael, Sandy Berrigan, Chuck Hathaway, Nancy Marie De Muri, Mike MacDonald, Martha Furey, Vicki Raymond Ford, Gae Walters Gargac, Billy & Shelly Kreutzmann, Bruce Black, Ray Rice, Ray Dahlin, George Doubiago, David Feinstein, Raul Volcan, Bill Pearlman, Johnny Dark, Alice Edens, Mozelle Strickland, Carl and

Vivian Zetterholm, Jim Dodge, Michael Nielsen, Sue and Herb Siegle, Kay Brown-Rogers, Ben Guerule, Bob and Nancy Harvey, Cathy Fischer, C.D. Wright, Beverly Clauser, Billy Jean Hicks, Marcelene Brogli, Cassandra Sagan, John Oliver Simon, Cole Swenson, Michael Larrain, Maureen Hurley, Toby Kaplan, Sierra and Crystal, Stella Monday, Neeli Cherkovski, Max Schwartz, Tom Dawson, Lawrence Ferlinghetti, Stephen Kessler, Pat Knox, Grace Brisky, Dan Propper, Norma Thomas, Kay Rudin, Hohu-seca-sica: Jack and Shirley Little, Deirdre Sharett, Elaine Eisenberg, Stephanie Mines, Lee Perron, Jo Fliege, Kendrick Peavy, Fara, Jim Hartz, William Pitt Root, Finn Wilcox, Pat Fitzgerald, Sam Hamill, Tree Swenson, Maryna Lawson, Cheryl Van Dyke, Judith Louise, Christine Pacosz, Kevin Aims, Kevin Quigley, Teresa and Dylan Fitzgerald, Dane and Shi-Shi Fitzgerald, D.J. Hamilton, Tim McNulty, Mary Morgan, Chuck Easton, Autumn Scott, Gary Lemmons, Jan Hill, Hank Tjemsland, Chellie Roberts, Jim Heynen, Carol Jane Bangs, Greg Lechtenberg, Marianne Ware, Jim Maynard, Monica Bregsgil, David Sharp, Margaret Lee, Karen Timberlake, Zelda Balchowsky, Barbara Berry, Bill Ransom, Leonard Randolf, Deborah Le Sueur, Bill O'Daley, Francisco X. Alarcon, Bob Vincent, Paul Reynolds, Walt McKeown, Georgia Richards, Douglas Spence, Laurie Graham Schieffelin, Linda Mason, Kate Estes, Barbara Morgan, Steve Johnson, Connie Weneicke, Carolyn Dry, Diane and Echo, Duke Rhoades, Bonnie Cullin, Rusty North, Jim Tortoff, David Romtvedt, Amigo Capouillez, Steve Helman, David Laven, George Tsongas; Roger Fontain, Robert Sund, Paul Hansen, Jennifer Clarke, Tony Bean and the others I have undoubtedly overlooked, to whom I extend my apologies and request for understanding.

Special acknowledgement to Meridel Le Sueur, John Crawford and Anya Achtenberg, to Jim Dochniak and to West End's editorial collective, including Mary McAnally, Teresa Anderson, Sue Ann Martinson, Joy Harjo, and Neala Schleuning;

and to the following places, institutions and/or other endeavors in which my poetry, particularly in public readings and/or in spirit, has been nourished: The Greenwood Pier Cafe, Mendocino Art Center, KMFB (Fort Bragg), The Well, Garbo's Sleeping Lady Cafe, Intersection, Centrum, The Longest Walk, Midwest Villages and Voices, The Seagull, Casper Inn, The Oasis, Mendocino Hotel, Dick's, the employees and customers of the Port Townsend Sea Gallery, The Town Tavern, The Log Cabin, the communities of the Mendocino coast, North Beach, Ramona, Ashland and Port Townsend, Country Woman Magazine, The Pennebaker Electric Blues Harmony Band, Roses, Horse Badorties, The Grateful Dead, the very fine musicians of the Mendocino Coast and the Olympic Peninsula.

This volume is published in an edition of 1200 copies.
It was designed, typeset and keylined by Jim Dochniak in Minneapolis,
with cover design by Tree Swenson of Port Townsend, Washington.
Type is 11 point Baskerville.

58 075